Coac
Driver's

Croner
a Wolters Kluwer business

Wolters Kluwer (UK) Limited
145 London Road
Kingston upon Thames
Surrey KT2 6SR
Tel: 020 8247 1175

Published by
Wolters Kluwer (UK) Limited
145 London Road
Kingston upon Thames
Surrey KT2 6SR
Tel: 020 8247 1175

First published December 1987
Second Edition 1989
Third Edition 1993
Fourth Edition 1997
Fifth Edition 2004
Sixth Edition 2005
Seventh Edition 2006
Eighth Edition 2007
Ninth Edition 2008
Tenth Edition 2009
Eleventh Edition 2010
Twelfth Edition 2011
Thirteenth Edition 2012
Fourteenth Edition 2013

ISBN 978–1–85524–770–3

Printed by Gutenberg Press Ltd, Malta

Contents

INTRODUCTION

I feel honoured to have been asked to assume the role of Editor of the *Coach & Bus Driver's Handbook* for the benefit of today's passenger-carrying vehicle (PCV) drivers. In common with past editors, I have served my time in the bus and coach industry, in my case over 40 years, and I hope that my contribution to this worthy publication will be well received and helpful in the day-to-day work of the professional coach and bus driver.

I must also thank Gordon Humphreys of Foster Tachographs, who has kindly undertaken the task of updating *Chapter 6* of the book which covers the critical area of working time and driver record keeping.

Demand for previous editions shows that there is an ongoing need for this book, which — although of value to all UK Passenger Carrying Vehicle drivers — is targeted mainly at employees of small to medium-sized fleets and owner/operators.

The road passenger transport industry continues to be heavily regulated and the associated legislation places ever-growing demands on both operators and drivers of PCVs. This *Handbook* gives priority to the requirements of the driver in this respect, especially with regard to the enormous responsibility of carrying passengers in comfort and safety.

The aim of the *Handbook* is to assist all coach and bus drivers by providing a comprehensive cross-section of the new and ever-changing rules in plain language. However, the main emphasis is placed upon the knowledge required for legal, safe and efficient operation of PCVs. Where the term "driver" is used throughout it refers to the professional drivers of buses and coaches operated for hire or reward under the authority of an operator's licence ("O" licence).

This 14th edition of *Coach & Bus Driver's Handbook* for 2013/14 charts numerous legislative changes that have been implemented over the past 12 months since the previous edition. The volume of updating required for this edition reflects the fact that this has again been a year of significant change; change prompted by both domestic and European legislative developments, as well as by the continued modernisation and investment on the part of the industry itself.

By the time this book is published, the Certificate of Professional Competence for passenger vehicle drivers will be fully integrated into industry practice, and will be operating alongside revised driving licence regulations that have largely harmonised EU practice since early 2013. These changes are reflected in *Chapter 3*. As indicated above, the chapter on working time has also been overhauled.

Numerous other changes and developments which affect operators and their drivers on a day-to-day basis have been incorporated in this edition of the book, including the replacement of the Criminal Records Bureau by the Disclosure and Barring Service; changes to industry financing (BSOG); and to the regulatory regime (OCRS).

As ever, in order to keep the text to reasonable "pocketbook" proportions, detailed references to European directives, UK Acts of Parliament and Statutory Instruments are omitted. Should readers wish to expand their knowledge in this respect, the use of the more detailed reference companion, *Croner's Coach & Bus Operations*, is highly recommended.

It should be noted that some Acts of Parliament do not extend to Northern Ireland and operators based there or in the Channel Islands or the Isle of Man are subject to different law.

The coach and bus operating industry in Great Britain continues to hold a proud passenger safety record and I hope that my contribution to driver professionalism, via this *Handbook*, will help to keep this record in place. Drivers who find the *Handbook* of particular interest might wish to consider studying the subject of coach and bus operations in greater depth with a view to enhancing their role and future involvement in this fascinating business.

Ian Barlex FIC CMC MInst TA

Note: Transport law is constantly changing. The contents of this *Handbook* are correct at the time of printing.

September 2013

1 OPERATORS' LICENCES

Before any person or operating firm can legally use a vehicle with nine or more passenger seats to carry passengers for hire or reward, they must hold a public service vehicle (PSV) operator's licence ("O" licence). This is granted by the Traffic Commissioner for the local Traffic Area, who is the issuing authority for both goods and PSV "O" licences. (See the Vehicle and Operator Services Agency (VOSA) website *www.gov.uk/vosa* for details or email: enquiries@vosa.gov.uk.)

Hire or reward operation in this context includes both carriage at separate fares and carriage of a party of people at a composite fare (private hire).

The term "separate fare" covers all payments made by individual passengers, even if not made directly to the driver or operator. For example, an admission ticket for an event which confers a right to be carried on a vehicle to and from the event will be a "separate fare" and the operator will require a PSV "O" licence.

It may help to explain the distinction between the PSV and PCV terms. The latter is terminology used in driver licensing rules to describe vehicles with nine or more passenger seats. Dependent on the circumstances, a bus can simultaneously be classified as being both a PSV (because of its hire or reward work) and a PCV (because of its size).

Where free transport is provided for employees — for example, by a firm with its own minibus or personnel carrier — an "O" licence is not needed. But where a business, such as a hotel, uses a passenger-carrying vehicle (PCV) as a "courtesy coach" in connection with its main business activities this is classed as hire or reward operation and the operator must hold an "O" licence.

Any vehicle with eight or fewer passenger seats that is operated by an "O" licence-holder to carry passengers at separate fares, and which would otherwise be exempt, must also be included on that operator's PSV "O" licence.

CAR-SHARING

The practice of sharing a car or van with eight or fewer seats — for example, by employees commuting to and from the same workplace — is largely permitted, provided the fare or fares paid total no more than the running costs of the vehicle, including depreciation. In such cases, the vehicle is not a PSV, nor is the driver's insurance normally invalidated by virtue of a "private" vehicle being used "commercially" in this way.

GROUP HIRE AND USE OF STRETCH LIMOUSINES

Where a party hires a coach, bus or limousine from an operator for a lump sum and then shares the cost among its members by charging separate fares, technically even if the vehicle has eight or fewer seats it will be a PSV. In the case of limousines (stretched) with nine or more passenger seats, these vehicles must be approved by VOSA before they can be operated as a PSV.

Note: More detailed information on the operation of stretch limousines may be found in the VOSA booklet *Guidance for Operators of Stretch Limousines* (published in March 2011) obtainable free via the VOSA website at *www.gov.uk/vosa*.

However, operation of privately organised trips at separate fares is widespread and many coach drivers convey such parties on a regular basis. To regularise the practice, the **Public Passenger Vehicles Act 1981** provides that the hire will not be construed as carriage at separate fares if the following conditions are met.

- Neither the driver, owner nor operator of the vehicle made the arrangements for bringing the party together.

- The journey has not been previously advertised to the public at large, except by a notice displayed at a place of work, a church or a club, or in a journal circulating mainly among the relevant employees, worshippers or club members.
- All passengers make substantially the same journey and there are no fare differences according to time or distance travelled.

TYPES OF PSV "O" LICENCE

There are three types of PSV "O" licence issued by Traffic Commissioners. They are:

- standard licences for national and international operations (with green windscreen discs)
- standard licences for national operations only (with blue windscreen discs)
- restricted licences for ancillary use of PSVs with up to 16 passenger seats (with orange windscreen discs).

In addition, Traffic Commissioners can issue Community Bus permits and permits for "welfare vehicles" (these latter can also be issued by local authorities and other "designated bodies").

Standard "O" Licences

These allow the operation of any size of PSV. Before the granting of a licence, the operator has to satisfy the Traffic Commissioner that it:

- has sufficient financial resources to operate the vehicles safely — the operator can elect either to maintain them in person in its own facilities or to contract out the maintenance, but if it is contracted out the operator remains responsible for the condition of the vehicles on the road
- is of "good repute", ie free of previous convictions relating to the use of a PSV during the last five years; in particular, convictions for a serious offence where a sentence of imprisonment for a term exceeding three months, a fine

exceeding level 4 (£2500) on the Standard Scale, or a community service order for more than 60 hours, was imposed

- is professionally competent, or employs a professionally competent transport manager. The professionally competent person must hold a PSV Certificate of Professional Competence (CPC).

  Note: The CPC referred to above, which is applicable to transport managers — ie *not* PSV drivers — has been merged into a single professional competence qualification since 4 December 2011. While national and international qualifications and licences continue for existing holders, any newly qualified managers will have international status. The previous OCR official separate manager CPC examinations have been merged into a single examination. An alternative examination route is now available via CILT.

These CPCs are not to be confused with the Driver CPC.

Traffic Commissioners may suspend, curtail or revoke a PSV "O" licence for breaches of the regulations concerning drivers' hours and records, mechanical condition of the vehicle or contravention of any conditions attached to the licence.

Restricted Licences

An operator may have a restricted licence which covers passenger vehicles with 8 or fewer passenger seats, or PSVs with 9–16 seats, exclusive of the driver's seat, which are used non-commercially. (See comment below, defining "non-commercially".) No more than two vehicles per restricted "O" licence may be authorised.

"Non-commercially" in this context is different than in the context of car-sharing or permit operation and means any operation which is otherwise than in the course of a business of carrying passengers, or a business conducted by a person whose main occupation is not the operation of PSVs with more than eight seats. This would include, for example, the use of a minibus by a taxi firm, whose main business is not PSV operation and whose taxis have eight or fewer seats, or a hotelier whose business is accommodating guests, not carrying passengers. Taxi operators are major users of restricted licences. The holder of a restricted licence does not have to prove professional competence.

Special Restricted "O" Licences

These are issued by Traffic Commissioners to holders of taxi (hackney carriage) licences and private hire cars who apply to run a registered local service. There are no requirements as to good repute, financial standing, or professional competence although the holder has to satisfy the local authority's licensing officer that he or she is a fit person to hold a taxi or private hire vehicle licence and that the vehicle to be used meets prescribed safety standards.

Traffic Commissioners may attach to a special restricted licence a condition that it be used as a PSV only to run a registered local service from or within the area of the appropriate local licensing authority. When the vehicle is used as a PSV the driver will come within the scope of the domestic drivers' hours regulations (see *Chapter 6, Drivers' Hours, Working Time and Tachograph Legislation*) but will not need to hold a PCV category driving licence.

Permits

These were introduced to enable voluntary and non-profit making groups to undertake PSV work without the need for an "O" licence. They mainly involve minibuses but with the Traffic Commissioner's approval, vehicles seating 17 and more passengers can be used. Large vehicles must comply fully with PSV maintenance and inspection standards and the driver must observe the EU drivers' hours rules and tachograph requirements. Drivers must have category D entitlement.

They are of two types, known by reference to the sections of the **Transport Act 1985** which established them:

- Section 19 permits — for closed groups of users or members
- Section 22 permits — often village ventures born out of the need to provide a public bus service.

In addition to the Traffic Commissioners, s.19 permits may be granted by designated bodies (eg local authorities, national charities or church organisations).

S.19 Minibus permits

Designated bodies as described above may issue such permits only to operators of small buses.

Permit vehicles, which are used mainly by voluntary organisations such as community transport, schools and colleges, and social welfare and religious groups, may be used to carry passengers for hire or reward provided that:

- the organisation holding the permit operates the vehicles
- they are not available to the public at large
- they are being used non-commercially (ie not for profit)
- they are being used in accordance with any conditions on the permit.

Drivers of such vehicles must either:

- hold a full category D1 driving entitlement (and be at least 18 years of age), or
- be a volunteer over the age of 21 years, have held a full category B entitlement for a minimum of 2 years, and be driving the vehicle for social purposes only.

The maximum authorised mass (laden weight) of the minibus (excluding tail lift if fitted) must not exceed 3.5 tonnes gross vehicle weight (gvw).

A "Permit" disc must be displayed on the vehicle.

S.22 Community Bus permits

A Community Bus is a vehicle operated by a group or groups of persons concerned with the social and welfare needs of a community. Traffic Commissioners can issue Community Bus permits to allow the operators to provide a local service on a non-commercial basis and to carry passengers in other circumstances (eg private hire) to provide revenue to support the Community Bus service.

A paid driver needs appropriate PCV entitlement but for small vehicles a driver of a Community Bus can be a volunteer aged 21 years or over (or 18 years or over if holding an appropriate full PCV driving entitlement) but may not receive any payment other than expenses (including loss of earnings). In such circumstances a category B (car) licence will suffice. A Community Bus disc must be displayed on the vehicle.

Any local service provided for the public at large by the Community Bus must be registered with the Traffic Commissioners or, in London, provided under a London Local Service Permit issued by Transport for London (TfL).

Note: Drivers aged 18 or over with category D entitlement can drive a large "Permit" (or indeed any) bus with 17 or more passenger seats provided it is on a regular service not exceeding 50km route length.

"O" LICENCE CONDITIONS

Exemptions

Some PCVs need not be operated under a PSV "O" licence. These include local authority school buses (even when also available to the public at large), and buses and minibuses operated non-commercially by social, welfare, religious and educational organisations under a permit.

Issue of Licences

PSV "O" licences are issued in the operator's name and do not identify the vehicles that are used under them. The operator receives non-specific licence discs for the number of vehicles in the fleet and these must be displayed on each vehicle (in the windscreen).

Number of Vehicles

The "O" licence will specify the total number of vehicles that can be operated by the licence-holder. However, additional vehicles may be temporarily hired in for not more than two weeks and these can display the licence disc of the operator from which they are hired. In this case the operator (not the hirer) remains the "user" of the vehicle, responsible for its legal and safe operation. Restricted licence-holders cannot hire large buses with more than 16 seats from standard licence-holders.

Enforcement Powers of Traffic Commissioners

Traffic Commissioners have the legal authority to suspend, curtail or revoke a PSV "O" licence for breaches of the regulations concerning drivers' hours and record keeping or the mechanical condition of vehicles, or for contravention of any conditions attached to the "O" licence.

2 RUNNING A LOCAL SERVICE

QUALITY CONTROL

Anyone holding a PSV "O" licence may, on giving due notice to the Traffic Commissioners, register and run a local bus service outside London. A service may be withdrawn on giving a similar period of notice.
Note: Notice requirements are different in Scotland.
Local authorities (LAs) running school buses, holders of Community Bus permits and operators of taxi and private hire vehicles who have obtained a special restricted PSV "O" licence may also register and operate a local bus service.

Competition

Thus, in the deregulated environment outside London, the operator of a local bus service, even if operating this under a service subsidy agreement for which it has successfully tendered, is completely unprotected against competition on the route.

Punctuality and Reliability

To aid improvements in the punctuality of local bus services, operators and local authorities are being encouraged by the Department for Transport (DfT) to form Bus Punctuality Improvement Partnerships. The partnerships must develop a Bus Punctuality Improvement Plan for their respective areas and demonstrate action towards achieving agreed objectives/targets and measurable improvements in the quality and reliability of bus services.

Powers of Traffic Commissioners

Traffic Commissioners require local bus services to be operated in accordance with registered details and to be operated on time. They have powers to stop an operator running a local service and/or impose a financial penalty if the operator fails to run the services on time or at all, or if the operator or an employee can be shown to have "intentionally" interfered in the running of another operator's local service. "On time" has been defined by the Traffic Commissioners as any time within a "six-minute window" of one minute ahead/five minutes behind scheduled arrival/departure time. Under new monitoring arrangements introduced in 2012, VOSA officials are checking that operators have procedures in place for the proactive management of punctuality.

Drivers' Behaviour on the Road

It is, therefore, imperative that drivers behave responsibly and do nothing to jeopardise their employer's licence. Competition can only be met legitimately on quality of service, so reliability, timekeeping, good driving and attention to passengers' needs are essential.

LOCAL SERVICES

Quality Partnership and Quality Contract Schemes

Under the **Transport Act 2000**, Local Transport Authorities (LTAs) in England and Wales are given powers to introduce Quality Partnership (QP) and Quality Contract (QC) schemes. The former restrict the provision of local services to those operators that meet certain standards determined by the LTA in exchange for facilities provided by the LTA. QC schemes go even further and are capable of giving exclusive rights to run services under a tendering process. In either case, the freedom afforded by the **Transport Act 1985** is severely reduced or even removed.

The **Transport Act 2000** along with the **Transport (Scotland) Act 2001** allow LTAs to force operators to be part of multi-operator ticketing schemes and also empower LTAs to provide information to the public on transport services and to charge operators the cost of so doing.

Local Services (Except London)

A local service is any service on which a passenger can travel a distance of not more than 15 miles measured in a straight line.

Local Services (In London)

Within Greater London, a local service can only be operated either by agreement with Transport for London (TfL) (such agreements usually result from successfully tendering to TfL for a service) or under a London Local Service Permit granted by TfL. These rules also apply to cross-boundary services entering, and stopping in, Greater London.

Timings

Once an operator has registered a local service it must be run strictly in accordance with the registration. Failure to do so, or operation of an unregistered service, can be sufficient reason for a Traffic Commissioner to impose a financial penalty or consider attaching a condition to the "O" licence preventing the operator from running that, or any other, local service.

Punctuality is important, so a driver always needs to know what the accurate time is. *Services should never be operated ahead of schedule.*

Retiming of School Journeys

Sometimes an operator is asked by a school to retime a journey (eg to accommodate an early finish or because of industrial action). This may be done if the service is a dedicated school service paid for by the LA, but only at the request of the LA and only for the purpose of enabling it to fulfil its duty to provide free school transport. If the timing of any other service on which school children rely is requested to be altered, the service must still be operated on its registered timing for the benefit of the public at large during the period of notification of the alteration to the Traffic Commissioner.

Duplication

Duplication of a local bus service is permitted but only to provide extra capacity over the whole or part of the route so long as the extra journeys are timed to operate as closely as possible to journeys in the registered timetable.

Traffic Regulation Conditions

Traffic Commissioners sometimes make traffic regulation conditions to reduce the risks of severe traffic congestion or prevent danger to road users or the public in general. These conditions may be attached to an "O" licence and drivers should be aware of them and observe them meticulously. A typical condition may be a ban on picking up or setting down in streets in the immediate vicinity of a bus station, in order to persuade operators to use the bus station and not cause congestion on its approaches. Other examples include controls on vehicle exhaust emissions and noise levels, eg from loudspeaker systems on vehicles.

Bus Stations and Bus Stops

Bus stations are usually operated by Integrated Transport Authorities (ITAs) or local authorities, although some remain in private hands. Bus station operators can levy departure charges and allocate stands, although they are legally required to do so as fairly as possible and not to favour any particular operator. Drivers should co-operate with ITA and local authority staff when using bus stations. In particular they should be prepared to move their vehicle from a stand if asked to do so and should avoid interfering with the manoeuvring of competitors' vehicles in the bus station. If their freedom of movement is compromised they should inform both the bus station operator and their employer.

Bus stops are the responsibility of the local highway authority (English shire counties or unitary authorities; Scottish and Welsh Governments and unitary authorities) and, in metropolitan areas, the ITA. Highway authorities may also make local traffic regulation orders, for example, to control picking up and setting down points for excursions and tours, or to limit layover time at city centre kerbside stops.

Hail and Ride

"Hail and ride" services do not observe bus stops but pick up passengers on being hailed and set them down on request. Drivers on such services must only observe hail and ride working on those sections of the route which the Traffic Commissioner has approved for that purpose. When driving a hail and ride service it is more important than ever to be on the lookout for intending passengers and to show courtesy to other road users by avoiding sudden and unsignalled stops, or stopping at dangerous points such as on the brow of a hill, or in proximity to a road junction or on a bend.

Faretables, Timetables and Destination Notices

Operators must display on a vehicle used on a registered service, or make available on such a vehicle:

- the faretable
- the timetable.

Destination and route number indicators must be displayed correctly and clearly to the exterior of a vehicle used on a registered service.

These conditions do not apply to excursions and tours.

Taxis

A taxi or private hire car may register and run a local service if the operator has obtained a special restricted "O" licence. (Taxis and private hire cars are vehicles with fewer than nine passenger seats, licensed by a local authority.)

In addition, taxis may be hired at separate fares from authorised places, ie specially designated ranks, at which taxis to common destinations may ply for hire. They must display a "Shared Taxi" sign, and *may not* ply for hire at separate fares by cruising along a bus route but the driver may "tout" for business at the designated ranks. He or she must do so in an orderly way, by word of mouth only, and within six metres of the taxi.

Taxis and private hire cars may also be pre-booked at separate fares.

Drivers of PSVs should not interfere with taxi operators but may report any transgressors of the above rules to the local taxi licensing officer, or, in the case of the operator of a taxi or bus running a local service, to the Traffic Commissioner.

Bus Service Operators Grant

Operators of local services in England and Scotland receive rebates of fuel tax under a scheme currently known as the Bus Service Operators Grant (BSOG). If the Traffic Commissioner finds that any operator has intentionally interfered in the operation of another operator's local service, or failed to operate a local service as registered, or run an unregistered local service, then the Commissioner has powers under the **Transport Act 1985** and **Transport Act 2000** (as amended) to apply one or both of the following penalties:

- the prohibition of the operation of a specified or any local service
- the payment of sums up to £550 per vehicle used under the operator's "O" licence.

Under the Government's Comprehensive Spending Review the BSOG was reduced in England by 20% from 1 April 2012. Further changes will be applied in England with effect from October 2013. In Scotland, the basis of payment was altered with effect from 1 April 2012. In Wales, BSOG has been replaced with effect from 1 April 2013 by the Regional Transport Services Grant (RTSG), administered by Welsh Regional Transport Consortia.

COMPETITION LAW

Competition law applies to the bus industry in exactly the same way as it applies to retailers in the high street.

Any agreement made between two or more operators in which they voluntarily accept restrictions on their ability to compete must be registered with, and comes under the scrutiny of, the Office of Fair Trading (OFT). This will include any agreements on joint operations, tendering, ticketing or route-sharing. The OFT may of course decide that the agreement is not potentially harmful to the public or designed to exclude a competitor and permit it.

Unfair competitive practices, especially the practice known as "predatory pricing" where a large operator drops bus fares to an uneconomic level to drive a competitor off "its" route, can also be investigated by the OFT.

Drivers should be on the look-out for restrictive and anti-competitive practices and report these to their employers, or complain to the OFT.

TENDERED SERVICES

Schools contracts are often seen as a small operator's bread and butter income. These, together with any socially desirable services which no operator has registered because takings are too low, are put out to tender by county and unitary councils and passenger transport executives (PTEs) (in metropolitan areas).

Drivers operating tendered services should be especially vigilant to ensure that no journeys are lost and must report any lost mileage immediately. Failure to do so can result in loss of the service subsidy contract.

Some tenders are won on the basis of quoting for a service operating cost with the tendering authority retaining the income from passenger fares (revenue). In such instances drivers must be able to account fully for all revenue, especially if their vehicle is boarded by a tendering authority's inspector.

CONCESSIONARY FARES

In addition to the national schemes, county and unitary councils and, in metropolitan areas, PTEs, have powers to extend concessionary fares schemes for pensioners, children under 17, scholars aged 17–19, and blind and disabled persons. These may take the form of free travel, tokens, or permits allowing reduced fares either all day or at off-peak times.

The above authorities also have powers to serve compulsory participation notices upon operators providing local services in their area.

Drivers should familiarise themselves with their local concessionary fares schemes and co-operate in operating them. In particular they must permit inspectors and data collectors employed by the above authorities to board their buses to make fare checks and collect data.

DEMAND RESPONSIVE TRANSPORT

Vehicles operated by some Community Transport organisations do carry passengers at separate fares. However, drivers should be aware that services such as Disabled Dial-a-Ride are not in competition since:

- they are not available to the public at large
- they are operated under the minibus permit regulations, and
- they are frequently subsidised by the local authority or PTE.

Such operations are allowed by virtue of operator's "Section 19" Permits (**Transport Act 1985**).

S.22 COMMUNITY BUSES

Community Bus services provide registered local services running to a published timetable and available to the general public in the same way as a local service operated under an "O" licence.

"Community Bus" operators are authorised by virtue of an operator's "Section 22" Permit (see *Permits*, p.9).

SCHEDULES AND DUTIES

Driving on a public passenger transport service is not a "nine-to-five" job and inevitably involves working unsocial hours.

In the case of some local urban and inter-urban services the first vehicle often leaves the depot before dawn and the last vehicle arrives back at the depot close to midnight. In express service operation, nights out for both vehicles and crews are not uncommon.

Scheduling a fleet of vehicles and allocating staff to them so as to provide the best service in the most economical manner is an art. The scheduler, often with computer assistance, produces an interdependent set of timetables, individual vehicle timings, a duty roster and a rota of individuals' daily duties.

Drivers do not need to be able to prepare these documents but it is essential that they can read and understand them. The smooth working of the undertaking relies on staff reporting for duty punctually, relieving earlier drivers or crews at the right time and following the instructions on the driver duty or vehicle running board regarding the operation of the service(s).

Schedules affect not only drivers' working lives but their social and domestic lives as well. Workable schedules and rotas which staff perceive to be "fair" improve drivers' working conditions and help retain a satisfied and well-motivated workforce. This, in turn, leads to a better and more reliable service to the public and enhances employees' job security.

The Service Timetable

Many operators issue their drivers with copies of the service timetables that they also make available to the public. In any case, one of the conditions attached to registration of a local service is that the timetable and faretable are carried or displayed on the vehicle.

Often the vehicle duty board will only show timings at route termini and perhaps one or two main points en route and the service timetable is then the only means the driver has of knowing his or her expected time at intermediate points.

Delays to services are often inescapable but running ahead of time is inexcusable. Apart from possible disciplinary action against the driver, early running can result in loss of revenue through missed passengers, loss of passenger goodwill, or the danger that the undertaking is reported to the Traffic Commissioners for failing to provide a service as registered, which could lead to sanctions against the "O" licence.

Drivers who are detailed to run a duplicate service should also be aware of, and try to comply with, the rules which Traffic Commissioners are applying to such services. These are that duplication should only take place to provide extra journeys over the whole or part of the route and that these journeys should be timed to run as closely as possible to the registered timetable.

Failure to comply with these simple rules could, wherever there is a competing service on the route, be construed as interference in the operation of another registered service.

The service timetable may employ either the 24-hour clock or am/pm timings.

Conventionally the timing points on the route are listed down a column at the left-hand side of the page and the timings for each journey are given in further columns to the right of this. Separate tables are prepared for journeys in either direction and sometimes for Saturdays, Sundays and bank holidays, or summer and winter services.

Codes at the head of each column give additional information. Standard abbreviations are M, T, W, Th, F, S, Su for the days of the week, plus the letters X for Excepted and O for Only, thus:

- MO = Mondays only
- NSSu = Saturdays and Sundays excepted.

Other letters and symbols are used to indicate journeys which operate:

- schooldays or college days only
- bank holidays only or excepted summer Sundays, etc.

Codes beside timings may indicate picking up and setting down restrictions, and timing information such as:

- u — stops to pick up only
- s — stops to set down only
- a — arrival time
- d — departure time.

Example of Typical Timetable for a Local Bus Service

STALYBRIDGE—OLDHAM									
Mondays to Saturdays									
	NS	NS			NS				
STALYBRIDGE, Bus Station	0715	0745	0845		1645	1715	1745		2245
Stamford Park	0718	0748	0848	AND	1648	1718	1748	AND	2248
Hurst Cross	0722	0752	0852	EVERY	1652	1722	1752	EVERY	2252
Abbeyhills, Welcome Inn	0730	0800	0900	HOUR	1700	1730	1756	HOUR	2256
OLDHAM, Town Square	0738	0808	0908	UNTIL	1708	1738	1808	UNTIL	2308

Sundays			
STALYBRIDGE, Bus Station	1345		2245
Stamford Park	1348	AND	2248
Hurst Cross	1352	EVERY	2252

Abbeyhills, Welcome Inn	1358	HOUR	2256
OLDHAM, Town Square	1408	UNTIL	2308

NS — Not Saturdays

A few undertakings issue non-conventional timetables with, for example, timings and timing points shown in rows rather than columns (see below), or with lists of departure times from main points with running times in minutes to intermediate points. While these are brief and less bulky than conventional timetables, they are also more difficult to use for both drivers and passengers.

Example of Timetable in Column Format

BUS STN	RAIL STN	NEAR TOWN	FAR TOWN
0900	0905	0915	0928
1000	1005	1015	1028
1100	1105	1115	1128
1200	1205	1215	1228
1300	1305	1315	1328

The Bus Running Board

While the service timetable shows all the journeys made by all the vehicles on the route, the running boards that may be prepared for each vehicle show only the specific journeys to be operated by that vehicle.

Since some service buses may be on the road for as long as 18 hours and may make journeys on more than one service, the same running board may be used in the course of a day by more than one driver. As it relates primarily to the work done by the bus, and only incidentally to some or all of the driver's duties, it should be left on the vehicle.

Running boards often contain a mass of information not shown on the service timetable, for example, descriptions of turning manoeuvres to be performed at termini, instructions to run "dead" or "out of service" between certain trips, or between depot and termini, or details of timed connections to be made (eg at a rail station).

Example of Running Board

Days of Operation	Leave Depot	Running Board No.
WEEKDAYS	0630	1

Service No.	1	1	2	2	1	1	2	2	1	1	2	2	1	1	2	2	1	1
BUS STATION	0625	0725	0730	0830	0835	0925	0930	1030	1035	1125	1130	1230	1235	1325	1330	1430	1435	1525
MOOR HILL	0658	0703	↓	↑	0858	0903	↓	↑	1058	1103	↓	↑	1258	1303	↓	↑	1458	1503
MILL GATE			0743	0818			0943	1018			1143	1218			1343	1418		
LITTLEFOLD			0758	0801			0958	1003			1158	1203			1358	1403		
Service No.	2	2	1	1	2	2	1	1	2	2	1	1	2	2	1	1		
BUS STATION	1530	1630	1635	1715	1730	1830	1835	1925	1930	2030	2035	2125	2130	2230	2235	2315	2330	
MOOR HILL	↓	↑	1658	1703	↓	↑	1858	1903	↓	↑	2058	2103	↓	↑	2258	2303	|	
MILL GATE	1543	1618			1743	1818			1943	2018			2143	2218			|	
LITTLEFOLD	1550	1603			1758	1803			1958	2003			2158	2203			|	
																	↓	
DEPOT																	2335	

From	To	Duty	
0630	1035	4	
1035	1330	3	
1330	1835	33	
1835	2335	11	

There are many different running board formats. Nowadays these are often computer print-outs. Usually, like the service timetable, they have timing points in the left-hand column, and timings of each trip in columns to the right of this. There the similarities end. Timings in both directions are usually shown, reading both up and down columns. Arrows are frequently used to indicate the direction of travel of the vehicle.

Some running boards have timing points at the head of each column and times in rows below these. A few operators produce running boards that could more accurately be described as "duty boards" since they contain details of all the trips to be performed by a driver working a specific period on duty. This type of board can be removed from one vehicle and taken to the next vehicle to be driven (perhaps after a meal break) since they are essentially a consolidation of extracts from the running boards of all the vehicles to be driven while working that duty.

There are a number of points that drivers can bear in mind when studying their running boards.

- *Interworking* — a vehicle may be switched from one route to another in order to maximise its productivity. For example, a works journey to an industrial estate may be linked with a following school journey from an adjacent housing estate.

  A more usual reason for switching vehicles between routes is to reduce the total number of vehicles required. Where two or more routes meet at a common point, such as a bus station, and the total of all the "layovers" or standing times of all the vehicles on the routes would be sufficient to perform a complete round trip, the vehicles may be rescheduled to interwork between the routes and thereby save a vehicle. It is important of course that a minimum agreed layover time still remains for each vehicle at its trip end.
- *Tidal flow operation* — at peak times when the majority of passengers are travelling in one direction, eg into town in the morning peak, it makes sense to maximise the number

of vehicles in service in that direction. Some vehicles can be scheduled to run empty back to outer termini "out of service" so as to be available there more quickly and perform an additional inward journey that will still be in the peak hour. For the sake of good passenger relations it is essential that the vehicle destination blinds on light trips clearly indicate that the vehicle is not in service.

- *Drop-back vehicles* — a vehicle may be brought out of depot to perform one round trip on a service and this journey may be included in part of a driver's duty. Although this is often done simply to duplicate journeys at times of peak demand, two other reasons for slotting a "drop-back" into a service are:
  - to enable a service affected by congestion to recover to its schedule timetable — the extra bus is slotted into the service at the start of the morning or evening peak and all buses on the route "drop back" to the timing of the following vehicle; by the time the extra bus has performed a round trip it will arrive back at the point where it was slotted in simultaneously with a service bus and one or other of the vehicles can be returned to depot
  - to cover meal breaks — the extra bus takes over the journey which the driver taking the meal break would have operated; all buses on the service then drop back as described above, enabling their drivers to take a meal break equivalent to the headway between vehicles (the drop-back bus or buses can be returned to depot when all meal breaks have been completed).

For example — if the round trip running time (including 5 minutes' layover at each end of the route) on a service run with four vehicles is 60 minutes, departures from the bus station could be as follows.

Bus No. 1	00 minutes past the hour
Bus No. 2	15 minutes past the hour
Bus No. 3	30 minutes past the hour
Bus No. 4	45 minutes past the hour

Bus No. 1   00 minutes past the next hour

Inserting an extra bus on the hour allows bus No. 1 to take over the 15 minutes past departure, No. 2 the 30 minutes past, etc. On the next hour, Bus No. 4 and the extra bus will arrive simultaneously at the bus station, and the extra bus or Bus No. 4 can be returned to the depot without destroying the basic 15-minute headway on the service.

- *Frequency changes* — lower frequencies are usually provided between peak periods, in the evenings and on Sundays. At the times when frequencies are changed the driver may notice that the pattern of departure times from termini alters. For example, with departures on the hour and every 20 minutes a change from three to two buses per hour will change the departures at 20 and 40 minutes past the hour to one at half past the hour.
- *Differential running times* — while it is often difficult to run to time in the peak hours, it is also often frustrating for both drivers and passengers if time has to be spent in the off-peak waiting at timing points to avoid running early. For this reason the running times allowed on a route are often adjusted at different times of the day to take account of traffic congestion and heavier passenger loadings.

CREW ALLOCATION

The GB ("domestic") and EU drivers' hours rules and Working Time Regulations set an upper limit on the amount of work that can be allocated daily and weekly to drivers.

Daily Limits

The maximum length of time for which a driver on domestic rules journeys and work (which includes most regular local services) can drive without taking a break of at least 30 minutes is 5½ hours. This may be extended to 8½ hours if the combined total of all the breaks in that period is not less than 45 minutes. The driver must in addition have a break of at least 30 minutes at the end of this period unless it is the end of the working day. The maximum total driving time is 10 hours. The working day must not exceed 16 hours and the driver must normally have 10 hours' rest between working days; this may be reduced to 8½ hours on three occasions in each week.

On duties regulated by the EU drivers' hours (mainly longer-distance, private hire and touring work) the maximum aggregate driving time without a break (or breaks) of at least (or amounting to) 45 minutes is 4½ hours. This 45-minute break may be replaced by one break of 15 minutes followed by another break of at least 30 minutes distributed over the 4½-hour period. Breaks of less than 15 minutes' duration do not count towards an official 15 or 30-minute break.

The maximum total daily driving time is normally 9 hours but can be 10 hours twice in a fixed week. The driver must have 11 hours' rest in every 24 hours; this may be reduced to nine hours on three occasions between any two weekly rest periods. The minimum daily rest if the vehicle is multi-manned is 9 hours in every 30 hours.

Weekly Limits

Domestic hours drivers must have a fortnightly rest period of 24 hours off duty (ie in any two consecutive fixed weeks), and EU hours drivers must have a weekly rest of 45 hours no later than 144 hours after the last weekly rest, although there are reductions to this rule.

All drivers are entitled under the Working Time Regulations to limit their maximum average weekly working time to 48 hours. Domestic hours drivers can "opt out" of this limit by agreement with their employers but drivers who work under the EU hours rules cannot opt out.

The above is a necessarily brief résumé of the drivers' hours limits which affect the allocation of drivers and crews to vehicles. Full details are given in *Chapter 6*.

In addition to statutory limits on hours of work, many drivers are covered by trade union agreements which also affect their duties. These generally cover matters outside the statutory limits, such as the maximum number of "split" duties to be included within a roster, travelling times between relief points, and the place where meal breaks are taken.

Driving Duties

Duties are usually arranged in such a way that a driver is allocated to a vehicle in service for a portion of its time on the road before being relieved for a meal break. After the meal break the driver is then allocated to another vehicle for the remainder of his or her time "on duty" or "shift".

Overtime

In making up duties or "shifts", schedulers sometimes leave small portions of work unallocated, to be staffed on an overtime basis.

Allocators (or schedulers) and drivers have a duty to ensure that in detailing a driver to, or volunteering for, such an overtime portion, none of the following statutory limits is exceeded or encroached upon:

- maximum daily driving time
- daily spreadover
- minimum daily rest periods
- minimum weekly or fortnightly rest periods
- maximum average weekly "working time" limit
- "reference periods"
- "mixed", domestic or EU driving where these circumstances apply (see *Chapter 6*).

Some undertakings have negotiated standard weekly payments for drivers which equate with an average week's work on a roster containing some scheduled overtime. The rosters are arranged to even out the work done over a fixed period. Rest day working (see below) is usually still voluntary and not included in this averaging.

Types of Duty

To cover all the services in a full working day some staff will have to start work early and could be coming off duty even before midday; others will have to start late and work through to nearly midnight; and yet others will be needed to cover the work in the middle of the day. In urban areas, night services may also be operated. In addition, because there will be extra vehicles out in the morning and evening peaks, some staff will need to perform split duties, with a period of off duty between their two periods of work. A roster or "rota" (see below) is drawn up and posted well in advance to spread this work on a rotating basis and to acquaint staff with their personal duty patterns for the coming months.

Trade union agreements usually define different types of duties in some way so that allocators and staff know the time boundaries within which they are working. A typical agreement would be:

Early duty:	Finishing no later than 1530
Middle duty:	Finishing no later than 2000
Late duty:	Finishing after 2000
Split duty:	Covering two work portions (usually in the morning and evening peak periods) and with an intermediate off-duty period. This may be "paid through" and be of some duration between maximum and minimum limits, eg over 1½ but under 4 hours.

THE DEPOT'S DAILY DUTY ROTA

Size of the Rota

An estimate of the number of duties that will have to be worked by the staff at a depot in order to drive all the vehicles in service can be made by dividing the total number of bus hours by the average work content (ie ignoring signing-on and off times, meal breaks and any time spent by a driver travelling on foot or as a passenger to take over a bus).

Linking portions of work together in the most economic way so as to get the most productivity from bus drivers or crews is a skill, nowadays often computer-aided, the result being the list of numbered duties which are posted in the depot, usually in strict order of their starting times.

A typical duty extract on a rota may look like this.

Extract from Duty Rota

Duty No.	Sign On	Take-over		Bus No.	Relieved		Sign Off	Hours	Pay
		Time	Place		Time	Place			
M.1	1210	1230	Bus Stn	3	1615	Bus Stn			
		1645	Bus Stn	2	1940	Bus Stn			
		1945	Stand 1	4	1950	Ga-rage	2000	7.50	8.00

Note: M.1 — this is classed as a middle duty.
Sign on 1210 — including signing-on time allowance to enable the driver to collect a ticket machine module, find, check and take over the bus allocated to running board 3, and if necessary set the destination blinds, there may be an additional travelling allowance to enable the driver to reach the take-over point if this is, as in this case, not the depot where he or she signs on.

1615 to 1645 — meal break and statutory break. Take over Bus No. 2 at 1645 in the bus station.

1940 to 1945 — take over Bus No. 4. The five minutes allowed may include a couple of minutes' travelling time to an adjacent stand, perhaps in the street outside the bus station.

1950 — both the bus and the driver return to depot. Ten minutes' signing-off allowance given.

7.50 — time from signing on to signing off.

8.00 — time value of the duty for payment purposes. In this case it probably represents a negotiated minimum day's pay.

Note: The meal break is also "paid through" in this case. In some organisations, "paid through" spreadover duties have been negotiated. In others, payment may be at time and a half because of factors like Sunday working, extra late finishing, etc.

Standby duties are also written into the rota so that the signing-on and off times can be known in advance. Usually these correspond roughly to the type of duty which the relief replaces in the roster pattern. Occasionally there are portions of duties which contain no work content (eg the second half of a late duty) and these may be marked on the rota with an instruction such as "Enquire" which indicates that the driver can be asked to stand by for that time period.

Sometimes if the depot is fully staffed and there are no obvious problems the allocator (or scheduler) or inspector may allow the driver to sign off without incurring any pay penalties.

It may even be in the interests of an allocator to sign a driver off early in order to bring him or her in early the next day without infringing his or her statutory daily rest allowance.

Drivers should note in this case that although they may be rostered and paid for working until late, so far as their statutory hours are concerned what counts is the time they are actually on duty, not the time they are rostered.

Duty Rosters

In the duty roster that accompanies the rota, staff are allocated a numbered duty for every day on which they are scheduled to work. Some rosters are for seven days with an allocated rest day (and the opportunity to work overtime on one rest day per fortnight on domestic work). Others are for five days with certain rest days "starred" to indicate the opportunity for overtime. (These are more common where the bulk of weekend work is performed by part-time staff.)

To comply with drivers' hours regulations and union agreements, rosters are usually drawn up so that a long weekend is scheduled each month and no late duty is followed by an early duty.

Some duties are "standby" duties to cover for sickness and absenteeism; others are "regular reliefs" to cover specific types of duty left uncovered by a driver or crew being scheduled for a rest day.

Roster length

The total number of daily duties in a week (ie five times the number of duties on the daily rota plus the Saturday and Sunday rota) divided by the length of the working week gives an indication of the size of the roster. For example, if there are 61 duties in a week and staff work five days, this will give a roster length of 13 weeks with four "spare" or standby duties.

The length of a roster can be reduced by splitting it — for example, by allocating a group of drivers to a restricted number of routes.

The number of split duties will also depend upon the severity of the peak hour demands in relation to the off-peak traffic, in particular the extent to which operating frequencies have to be increased in the peak, or additional traffic can be generated in the off-peak to avoid operating too many part-time vehicles.

Duty Postings

Name	Week numbers for weeks commencing:				
	May 4	May 11	May 18	May 25	etc
Smith	1	2	3	4	5
Jones	2	3	4	5	6
Wil-liams	3	4	5	6	7

Green	4	5	6	7	8
etc					

Finding your way around the duty rota and roster

Drivers normally work their way through the roster to which they are allocated. Thus, if in the current week a driver is on week 1 of the roster given as an example below, he or she will work late duties M–F and have S and Su off.

The following week he or she will work week 2, having M and Tu off (providing the monthly long weekend) and then commence early duties. Note that for the purposes of drivers' hours this prevents an early duty following a late duty the previous night.

The rota will contain details of the work content of all the duties, so that a driver allocated to M.1 on M and Tu of Week 4 will be able to ascertain that on those days he or she will sign on at 1210 and sign off at 2000.

A typical short (12-week) duty roster might look like below. This is an example, not a model of all rosters.

Each individual undertaking will have its own negotiated roster pattern which will contain only some of these features.

Duty schedules and rosters are complicated (see example below). They are also sometimes changed at short notice to accommodate traffic irregularities.

Duty Roster

Week no	M	T	W	Th	F	S	Su
1	L1	L1	L1	L1	L1	*	*
2	*	*	E1	E1	E1	E1	E1
3	E1	E1	*	R	S1	S1	*
4	M1	M1	R	*	*	L1	L1
5	L2	L2	L2	L2	L2	*	*
6	*	*	E2	E2	E2	E2	E2
7	E2	E2	*	S1	R	M1	*
8	S1	R	M1	*	*	L2	L2
9	L3	L3	L3	L3	L3	*	*

10	*	*	E3	E3	E3	E3	M1
11	E3	E3	*	M1	M1	R	*
12	R	S1	S1	*	*	L3	R

Key

* = day off
L = late duties (3 on M–S and 2 on Su)
M = middle duties (1 each day)
E = early duties (3 on M–S and 2 on Su)
S = split duties (1 on M–S)
R = standby or regular relief (1 on each day)
eg: the relief on week 12 could work the early on week 11 if necessary.

Note: If in any doubt as to the duties to be worked on the current or following days it is safer to ask than to risk missing a duty. Not only could this be a disciplinary matter, it might also affect the reliability of services and could in the long term affect the operator's reputation, "O" licence and commercial survival, and jeopardise the driver's own job security.

Flexible Bus Services

Since February 2004, operators have been permitted to register and provide local services that do not have to run to a strict pre-set timetable or route. These "flexible services" — defined as those that (a) serve one or more local communities or neighbourhoods within a specified geographical area, or (b) are so flexible that it is not practicable to identify in advance all the roads to be used at any given time (NB: there may be fixed sections of the route but the vast majority of the journey is flexibly routed) — may vary their routes in response to requests from pre-booked passengers who will be given approximate bus arrival/pick-up times by the operator. Although the services are provided predominantly for pre-booked passengers, the services can also carry passengers who wish to board at normal fixed stops along any stretch of fixed line of route, as long as there are seats available.

3 DRIVER TRAINING AND DRIVER LICENSING

GENERAL INFORMATION

Driver Certificate of Professional Competence

Since 10 September 2008, when the new EU Vocational Training Directive (2003/59/EC) came into effect, a prospective PCV driver needs to hold both a category D or D1 PCV driving licence, and a PCV Driver Certificate of Professional Competence (CPC).

What the directive requires

Existing PCV licence-holders The directive requires that pre-existing PCV driving licence-holders — as at the 10 September 2008 commencement date for the scheme — who seek to continue working as PCV drivers must undertake an approved course of "periodic" training by 10 September 2013, while being employed by a PCV operator. Without the training and proof of the Driver PCV CPC qualification, drivers will no longer be able to be employed as a PCV driver.

Non-PCV licence-holders Non-PCV driving licence-holders since 10 September 2008 have needed to undergo the specified "initial" training before taking the relevant tests to obtain a PCV driving licence and gaining employment as a PCV driver. This means taking and passing the combined theory and hazard perception tests and the practical driving test as well as undertaking the initial Driver CPC training before being allowed to take up PCV driving — see below.

Exemptions from the PCV Driver CPC

There are exemptions from the requirement for drivers to hold a PCV Driver CPC when driving certain PCVs, as follows.

- Drivers of "small buses" (those adapted to carry nine but not more than 16 passengers) under ss.19 and 22 permits (ie operated on a not-for-profit basis by charitable and other groups) who qualify to do so without holding PCV entitlement, are exempt from the requirement for a CPC qualification. If a driver of such vehicles does hold a PCV entitlement, the DfT recommends that he or she should be encouraged to gain the CPC qualification, but it is not mandatory to drive on permit work.
- Other exempt PCVs are those:
  - with a maximum authorised speed not exceeding 45kph (approximately 28mph)
  - used by, or under the control of, the armed forces, a police force or a fire and rescue authority
  - undergoing road tests for technical development, repair or maintenance purposes, or that are new or rebuilt vehicles that have not yet been put into service
  - used in a state of emergency or assigned to a rescue mission
  - used in the course of driving lessons for the purpose of enabling that person to obtain a driving licence or a Driver CPC
  - used for non-commercial carriage of passengers or goods for personal use
  - carrying material or equipment to be used by the driver in the course of his or her work, provided that driving that vehicle is not that person's principal activity.

Some PCV drivers may only occasionally drive under one or more of these exempt categories, in which case they can legally move in and out of the exemption, depending on the circumstances in which they are driving. For example, the DfT suggests that a bus mechanic would be exempt while driving a bus to check that it had been correctly repaired, but would need to hold a Driver CPC if he or she were also to drive a bus on a passenger-carrying service.

Training requirements

The training requirements for the Driver CPC are much broader and more complex than those previously required to obtain a PCV driving licence, and are aimed at improving road and passenger safety and passenger comfort, and reducing fuel consumption and environmental damage — as well as arousing young people's interest in a coach or bus-driving career and bringing an improved professional image to the industry.

The Driver CPC scheme is based on a system of approved methods of "initial" and "periodic" training and certification, provided by approved trainers and working within approved training centres. The training regime itself is as specified by the EU in the wide-ranging and quite complex list of topics indicated by the official syllabus to be found in the appendix at the back of this handbook.

Approval for trainers, training centres and training courses is given only by the Joint Approvals Unit for Periodic Training (JAUPT). For a current list of approved PCV CPC training centres visit *www.jaupt.org.uk*.

Initial training The "initial" training scheme — set at NVQ Level 2 — for those who do not yet hold a PCV licence amounts to four hours of theory tests and a two-hour practical driving test to obtain both the relevant PCV driving licence and the Driver CPC qualification.

- The basic driving licence theory test of 1½ hours plus 2½ hours of extra theory testing for the CPC makes 4 hours in total, comprising:
  - *Module 1a* — 100 multiple choice questions (MCQs) (85% pass mark required)
  - *Module 1b* — a 20-video-clip hazard perception test
  - *Module 2* — a number of theory test case studies (usually three) using diagrams, pictures and graphics as well as

text, in which the candidate is presented with a defined scenario on which questions will be based.

- The practical element of the test is made up of:
  - *Module 3* — a basic practical on-the-road driving test of 1½ hours
  - *Module 4* — half an hour of extra practical questioning; the so-called practical demonstration test (ie "tell me, show me" types of questions or tasks) for the CPC — making two hours in total.

This theory testing is undertaken at existing DSA driving theory test centres and is touch-screen-based where appropriate.

Periodic training Following the initial CPC training for new PCV drivers when first acquiring their PCV driving licence, as described above, these drivers and all pre-existing valid PCV licence-holders from that time onwards (ie 10 September 2008) will have to complete a course of "periodic" training by September 2013 in order to obtain and retain their Driver CPC qualification and their existing PCV licence. This training requirement will need to be met subsequently on a five-yearly basis.

The "periodic" training must be undertaken at an approved Driver CPC training centre (or at JAUPT-approved in-house training sessions) in sessions of at least 7 hours each (ie 7 hours of actual direct contact with the trainer within a 24-hour period) and amount in total over the 5 years to at least 35 hours of tuition. To achieve this training requirement, drivers could undertake one week at the start of the scheme or a full week at the end of the five-year period, or spread the training out on a day-by-day basis throughout the five years.

The training objective would be to provide:

- general "up-skilling" to improve overall driver performance and safety awareness
- specific training to account for, say, new technological developments in vehicle design
- skills in operating "best practices" as and when they occur.

Acquired rights

Pre-existing driving licence-holders at the date when the new scheme came into operation (ie 10 September 2008 for PCV licence-holders) are not required to undertake any initial tests to acquire a Driver CPC, as they have what is known as "acquired rights" (ie grandfather rights) and therefore are deemed to be "professionally competent" drivers — albeit without an actual Driver CPC document.

Note: This is a good reason why drivers should carry their driving licences with them at all times when driving — they may be asked for such evidence (see also below).

Pre-existing PCV licence-holders will obtain a Driver CPC on completion of their first 35-hour session of periodic training. This will then be renewed on completion of each subsequent five-yearly session of periodic training.

However, according to the Driving Standards Agency (DSA), a new session of periodic training should not be commenced until five years before the next expiry date of the driver's Driver Qualification Card. This will, potentially, leave a gap of a year or more in a driver's continuous professional development.

Drivers of "small buses" (those adapted to carry nine but not more than 16 passengers) under ss.19 and 22 permits (ie operated on a not-for-profit basis by charitable and other groups) who qualify to do so without holding PCV entitlement are exempt from the requirement for a CPC qualification. If a driver of such vehicles does hold a PCV entitlement, the DfT recommends that he or she should be encouraged to gain the CPC qualification, but it is not mandatory to drive on permit work.

Certification

Certification of the fact that a new driver holds the Driver CPC qualification will be by means of a Driver Qualification Card (DQC), made of plastic and credit card-sized. These cards are issued by the Driver and Vehicle Licensing Agency (DVLA) when a candidate meets the necessary qualification. In the meantime, PCV drivers who have not yet obtained their actual DQC will have evidence of their professional competence under grandfather rights, if such proof is required, by the date on their driving licence, which shows when their entitlement to drive PCVs came into effect.

A record of all driver training undertaken at approved centres is held on a central database by the DSA and it is on the basis of this record of training hours achieved that the DSA will notify the DVLA when to send the candidate his or her DQC. Drivers themselves may also check up on their own personal accumulated training hours by use of the DSA's new online driver enquiry service at *www.direct.gov.uk/checkdrivercpc*. Employers have the same facility, provided that they have the individual's permission to do so.

Cost of PCV driving tests

The cost of the tests for new PCV driving licence applicants (as described above) increased due to the longer tests involved. Since 5 October 2009 these fees are as follows.

Module 1a	Theory Test (ie 100 MCQs) = £35
Module 1b	Theory Test — Hazard Perception = £15
Module 2	Theory Test Case Studies = £30
Module 3	Practical (driving) Test = £115
Module 4	Practical Demonstration Test = £55

Replacements for lost or damaged DQCs cost £25 on issue. The fees for modules 3 and 4 increase to £141 and £63, respectively, if taken during evenings, weekends or bank holidays.

Minimum age for driving PCVs

A 20-year old with a Driver CPC qualification and full category D PCV entitlement may drive any category D operation. Such a driver should hold a DQC (driver qualification card) for driving commercially. A duly qualified 18-year old with a full category D may drive any regular service not exceeding 50km route length, and minibuses up to 16 passenger seats when holding D1 entitlement.

Driving tests

The established system of driver testing continues, with the number of theory test questions increased to 100 (with an 85% pass mark) and the hazard perception test to 20 video clips. The practical driving test remains at 1½ hours' duration but is supplemented by a series of questions that require the candidate to demonstrate their knowledge of vehicle safety matters.

Offences and penalties

Since 10 September 2008 all PCV drivers must carry evidence of their Driver CPC qualification and they risk being asked to produce this at the time of a roadside check.

- For pre-September 2008 PCV licence-holders the evidence will be the date on their vocational licence. PCV drivers should carry their driving licence at all times when actually driving, or when carrying out work that might involve PCV driving. It is an offence to fail to do so.
- For new PCV drivers from 10 September 2008 the evidence will be the DQC issued to them on satisfactory completion of the initial CPC training achieved in conjunction with their driving qualification. This card must also be carried at all times when driving as described above.

Failure by drivers to produce their DQC, or their driving licence with date evidence, on request by a VOSA enforcement officer or police officer may result in a fixed penalty fine of £30.

The more serious offence will be failure to have undergone the mandatory 35 hours of periodic training within the preceding five years. Whether through forgetfulness or deliberate avoidance of the training regime, an offending driver could be fined up to £1000 on conviction.

Driving abroad

Since the Driver CPC scheme applies throughout the whole of the EU, British drivers driving abroad must always carry with them their driving licence (showing evidence of their pre-September 2008 PCV driving qualification) or their DQC. They risk an on-the-spot penalty if found to be in breach of this requirement.

Minibus Driver Awareness Scheme (MiDAS) Training

The Minibus Driver Awareness Scheme (MiDAS) training is becoming a standard qualification for minibus drivers. Although it is not yet a mandatory requirement, drivers may not be accepted to drive accessible vehicles belonging to other organisations unless they have received appropriate training in minibus driving skills.

This training is highly recommended for all new drivers as it offers:

- enhanced passenger safety and comfort
- increased confidence and reduced stress on the minibus driver
- a better image for the employer organisation.

The MiDAS course involves:

- driving practice and tuition, normally lasting for approximately one hour and allowing the trainee to drive the vehicle under supervision, to gain on-road vehicle familiarisation
- a classroom-based training session of approximately three hours
- driver assessment against MiDAS standards.

Driver Licensing (Third EU Directive on Driving Licences)

The regulations on driving entitlements have been amended in line with the Third EU Directive on Driving Licences, with most changes in effect since 19 January 2013. The various different types (110) of driving licence existing within the recently expanded European Community are being reduced to a common EU-wide single model licence in plastic card format — similar to the current UK photocard licence but without the paper counterpart. A microchip in the card carries the minimum information specified at the time by the European Commission.

The definitions of vehicle categories for driving entitlement purposes are now aligned to EU vehicle type approval legislation and all new licences will recognise the new definitions. However, existing drivers have retained their existing entitlements under grandfather rights.

Minimum requirements for the driving test for each entitlement category have been introduced along with revised medical standards and driver training requirements.

Revised minimum age limits have been introduced for new licence applicants (in conjunction with the new Driver CPC described above) and the maximum validity of a new vocational, eg PCV, driving licence will be five years. Renewal will be subject to the driver concerned meeting the CPC qualification — via the periodic training regime, also described above — and the required medical standards on each renewal occasion. Every five years, drivers up to age 45 will be required to sign a declaration that they still comply with the medical standards. After age 45, drivers will be required to provide a medical examination report every five years in order to retain their entitlement to drive. This will now include a separate eyesight section.

Qualifying for a Licence

Currently a driving licence may be obtained if during the past two years the applicant has:

- held a full licence (which he or she has mislaid, for example)
- passed a driving test
- held a full licence issued in Northern Ireland, the Isle of Man or the Channel Islands
- held a full British external licence, full British Forces Licence, exchangeable licence or Community licence.

Types of Licence (Current)

- Provisional licence.
- Ordinary driving entitlement (category B).
- PCV driving entitlement (category D).
- LGV driving entitlement (category C).

- Visitor's driving licence.

A provisional licence for the relevant vehicle category must be obtained in order to take a vehicle on the road for the purpose of learning to drive and taking the regulation test.

The holder of a provisional licence may drive vehicles of a class authorised on that licence only when accompanied by, and under the supervision of, a qualified driver who must be at least 21 years of age and have held a relevant full licence or a combination of relevant licences for at least three years. The vehicle must display "L" plates.

Application forms for most types of provisional licence are obtainable from post offices and when completed should be sent to the Driver and Vehicle Licensing Agency (DVLA) in Swansea together with the appropriate fee (see *Cost and Duration of Licences*, p.48). However, this does not apply for a provisional PCV (category D) licence which is dealt with as a separate item in this section.

There are different categories of vehicles for driving licence purposes (classified A–Q) each entitling a driver to drive the vehicles in that class.

A test passed on a vehicle with automatic transmission restricts driving to that type of vehicle in that driving licence class. A further test must be taken before driving a vehicle in that class with manual transmission.

Provisional licence-holders must pass a written theory test and a screen-based video hazard perception test before taking the practical test for a full category B entitlement to drive motor vehicles up to 3.5 tonnes gross vehicle weight (gvw) or with fewer than nine passenger seats.

Once these tests have been passed and a full category B entitlement has been gained, the driver can then apply for a provisional licence to drive vehicles either in category D

(PCVs with more than eight passenger seats) or D1 (PCVs with between 9 and 16 passenger seats inclusive), or category C or C1 (large goods vehicles).

An application for a provisional licence must be made which also entails submitting a medical report. On passing a category D/D1 test, including the theory and hazard perception tests (which must be passed first) the driver is then allowed to drive large/small passenger vehicles respectively for hire or reward or otherwise (see *PCV Driving Test*, p.50).

New drivers holding only a category B entitlement may drive vehicles in category D1 on behalf of a non-commercial body under the following conditions.

- A full licence has been held for at least two years.
- The driver is aged 21 years or over.
- No payment or any other consideration is received other than out of pocket expenses.
- The vehicle is being driven for social purposes only.
- There is no trailer attached to the vehicle.
- The maximum authorised mass (MAM) of the vehicle does not exceed 3.5 tonnes (excluding specialised equipment used for disabled passengers), and does not exceed 4.25 tonnes in other circumstances.

It is an offence to drive a vehicle on a public road unless the driver holds the appropriate category of licence for that particular class of vehicle.

Towing trailers

Drivers wishing to tow heavy trailers (those weighing more than 750kg MAM) must hold a full licence for the type of rigid vehicle (tractor unit) concerned, before taking the practical driving test for the trailer licence category D + E or D1 + E licence.

Note: The terms "maximum authorised mass (MAM)", "gross vehicle weight (gvw)", "permissible maximum weight (pmw)" and the word "mass" all have the same meaning.

Cost and Duration of Licences

Car provisional licence (valid until the holder's 70th birthday) with conversion to full licence after passing driving test	£50 £67 for evening and weekend tests
Exchange licence when additional group of vehicles added	free
PCV Provisional Licence	free
Full PCV entitlement in exchange for provisional licence	free

Renewal and Replacement

A driving licence must be renewed on or before the date of expiry. No days of grace are allowed. However, most ordinary car driving licences (eg category B) are valid until the holder reaches 70 years of age. Renewal after this age is free of charge and each replacement licence will be valid for a three-yearly term. Licences lost or defaced may be replaced at a cost of £20.
Note: These fees are subject to change.

Production of Licence

A police officer can demand the production of a driving licence for examination and if it is not immediately available it is a defence to show that the driver:

- produced it at a police station of his or her choice within seven days, or
- produced it there as soon as possible, or
- failed to produce the licence before the day on which proceedings for not producing the licence were commenced, as it was not reasonably practicable.

Remember that a driver must have a current ordinary licence with PCV entitlement (where applicable), and this must be signed. This is a legal requirement.

PCV DRIVING ENTITLEMENT

UK driving licences are "unified", showing driving entitlements for all vehicles issued centrally by the DVLA, the licensing authority for the issue of all driving licences. However, Traffic Commissioners retain their disciplinary powers in relation to drivers of PSVs, ie "O"-licensed (hire or reward) vehicles.

The medical standards that must be met before being permitted to drive PCVs are higher than for standard licences, and even tougher standards apply in the instance of diabetes, epilepsy and restricted eyesight.

Regulations permitting diabetics to drive in certain circumstances (such as having had no episode of hypoglycaemia in the past 12 months, regularly test their blood glucose, and have no other complications) have been harmonised throughout the EU since November 2011.

Eyesight standards were amended in 2013, but some relaxations still apply for drivers who obtained their vocational entitlement before 1 January 1997, can show regular PCV driving before then, and were not involved in an eyesight-related accident in the previous 10 years.

Regulations regarding epilepsy were also amended in 2013. Persons are permitted to apply for a PCV entitlement under certain conditions, for example if they have had no attack for 10 years before the licence is granted, or if a seizure has been isolated and has not taken place in the past five years.

Persons suffering from these conditions are advised to check the detail of the regulations carefully and to seek the appropriate advice.

Medical reports are required on applying for a PCV entitlement or renewing a PCV entitlement from age 45 onwards. PCV entitlement is valid until age 45; thereafter renewals must be made every five years and annually from the age of 65. There is an obligation for licence-holders to notify the DVLA if an illness or disability is expected to last more than three months, or worsens, if this is likely to affect their driving.

Categories of PCV Entitlement

Category D	Large PCV with nine or more passenger seats (including articulated buses)
Category D+E	PCVs towing trailers over 750kg gvw
Category D1 and D1+E	PCVs (minibuses 9–16 passenger seats). D1+E is minibuses towing trailers over 750kg gvw

PCVs

The driving licence regulations no longer distinguish between PSVs and non-PSVs. All buses, whether or not used for hire or reward, are classed as PCVs. Thus a category D or D1 entitlement is required to drive a PCV not used for hire or reward, but a PSV with eight or fewer passenger seats can now be driven on a category B entitlement (which covers motor vehicles with eight or fewer passenger seats not exceeding 3.5t gvw). Drivers of school buses owned by LEAs require category D entitlement, but not drivers of Community or "Permit" minibuses.

PCV Driving Test

Drivers must hold a full category B entitlement before applying for a licence showing *provisional* category D, or D1, (PCV) entitlement. This requirement, called staging, effectively prevents the conduct of dual ordinary/vocational driving tests.

The application must be made to the DVLA and can be made up to three months in advance of the licence being required, accompanied by a medical report which must be signed by a doctor not more than four months prior to the date the licence is to take effect. A fee for the provisional licence will be payable (see *Cost and Duration of Licences*, p.48).

Application for a PCV driving test is made to the DSA and should be accompanied by the appropriate test fee. The test comprises a theory test, including the hazard perception test, and a practical test.

The test may be conducted by:

- a PCV examiner employed by the DSA
- an examiner employed by a PSV operator and approved by the DfT to carry out tests on behalf of that operator
- persons authorised by the armed forces, a fire brigade or police authority for employees engaged in driving their vehicles.

The examiner will test the applicant's competence and in particular will have regard to:

- knowledge of the *Highway Code*
- competence to drive the vehicle and, if necessary, couple and de-couple the trailer
- knowledge of components relating to the safety of the vehicle
- ability to demonstrate, describe or perform random technical checks on their test vehicle, relating to:
  - fluid levels
  - tyres and wheels
  - steering
  - brakes
  - lighting
  - audible warnings
  - instruments
  - air tanks
  - loading.

The PCV driving test currently comprises two hours of driving and practical testing, plus four hours of driving licence and CPC theory testing.

On passing the test a driver will have a full PCV driving entitlement once the DVLA receives:

- the test pass certificate
- the provisional category D licence (for addition of full entitlement).

Minimum Test Vehicles

A minimum test vehicle for a category D driving test must be fitted with externally mounted nearside and offside mirrors, a seat belt for the examiner's seat, a working tachograph and anti-lock brakes (ABS). It must be at least 10m long, at least 2.4m wide and capable of attaining a speed of 80kph on the level.

The same minimum test vehicle may be used for a category D + E driving test providing it is drawing a closed box trailer of at least 1250kg gvw and is at least 2.4m wide and 2m high. With effect from 30 September 2013, new rules will apply in respect of minimum test vehicles for classes D+E and D1+E, ie vehicles pulling trailers. Such vehicles will have to carry a minimum weight, the absence of which will invalidate the test and forfeit the fee. The same rules will apply to Driver CPC practical tests and periodic training.

A driver with provisional category D entitlement who passes a PCV driving test in a vehicle with 9–16 passenger seats will obtain a category D1 (9–16 passenger seats) PCV entitlement which will only entitle the driver to drive a passenger vehicle with no more than 16 passenger seats for hire or reward. Minimum test vehicles for category D1 tests must weigh at least 4t and be at least 5m in length. The speed and braking requirements are as for category D minimum test vehicles.

Preparation for the Tests

Applicants should study:

- the *Highway Code*
- *The Official DSA Guide to Driving Buses and Coaches*, available from The Stationery Office and most bookshops
- *The Official Theory Test for Drivers of Large Vehicles*, available from The Stationery Office and most bookshops.

They should also make sure they know the rules regarding:

- equipment which must by law be carried on a PSV
- conduct of drivers and passengers
- drivers' hours and records regulations

• drivers' responsibilities after an accident.

Test applicants should also have a working knowledge of the construction and main component parts of the vehicle, and its weight, height, width and length. They should make sure it is roadworthy, has sufficient fuel for the test, displays "L" plates front and rear, and has a road tax disc and a secure seat for the examiner. Applicants must bring their full driving licence and provisional PCV driving licence with them and be punctual.

Working knowledge of the vehicle is an EU requirement that is now a formal part of the test. Applicants are required to understand enough about the test vehicle to appreciate when it is unsafe to drive, to be alert to possible defects, and to be able to report verbally or in writing to a fitter or mechanic the repairs thought to be needed.

A driver may drive a PCV without supervision immediately on the strength of a pass certificate and the provisional driving entitlement.

Documents Required for Tests

Applicants must first pass the theory and hazard perception tests and, when attending for these, produce:

- an appropriate driving licence for the category of vehicle for which the test is required
- evidence of identity, ie a passport (provided they bear a signature and a photograph of the applicant).

On the successful completion of this test the applicant, when presenting him or herself for the practical test, must supply:

- a theory test "pass" certificate
- an appropriate driving licence (as above)
- evidence of identity (as above)
- an appropriate vehicle in which the test is to be conducted (see *Minimum Test Vehicles*, p.52).

The applicant must declare on the Driving Test Report form that the vehicle provided for the test is covered against third party risk insurance.

Badges

There is no longer any requirement for drivers to wear PSV licence number badges.

Minimum Ages for Drivers

The revised regulations effective from 19 January 2013 made a number of changes to vehicle categories and minimum age rules throughout the EU, although ages for most UK vocational licences are unchanged. The principal change affecting PCV licences is that the age at which an unrestricted licence (and hence a digital tachograph card) can be obtained is reduced from 21 to 20, although the minimum age at which it is permissible to drive outside the UK is increased from 21 to 24. Revised age limits for relevant categories are tabulated below.

Category	Minimum Age	Notes
D1	21	1, 2, 3, 4
D1+E	24	1, 2, 3, 4
D	24	1, 2, 3, 5
D+E	24	1, 2, 3, 5

Notes

1. 17 years if a member of the Armed Forces
2. 18 in the following circumstances:
   (a) if learning to drive or taking a PCV driving test or the Driver CPC Initial Qualification
   (b) having passed a PCV driving test and the Driver CPC initial qualification and driving on a regular service where the route does not exceed 50km, or not engaged in the carriage of passengers.
3. Persons over 21 can drive without restriction (providing that they have a Driver CPC), on any commercial service, including on the continent, on EU drivers' hours operations. In the UK and certain other EU and EEA countries, the age limit is 20 in these circumstances.

4. A category D1 entitlement issued before 1 January 1997 limits the holder to driving vehicles "not for hire or reward" unless a further driving test has been passed.
5. 18 in the following circumstances:
   (a) if learning to drive or taking a PCV driving test or the Driver CPC Initial Qualification
   (b) having passed a PCV driving test and the Driver CPC initial qualification and driving under any of the following conditions:
      (i) on a regular service where the route does not exceed 50km
      (ii) not engaged in the carriage of passengers
      (iii) driving a vehicle of class D1.

Control Overview

Drivers should be aware of the enforcement regime that applies to road transport operations as follows:

- Secretary of State for Transport
  - Parliamentary Under Secretaries of State for Transport
- Traffic Commissioners
  - Deputy Traffic Commissioners
- VOSA
  - Vehicle Examiners
  - Traffic Examiners
- Police
  - Authorised Inspecting Officers
  - Police Constables
- Highways Agency Traffic Officers
- Trading Standards Officers (ie Weights and Measures Officers)
- Environmental Health Officers
- Health and Safety Inspectors
- HM Customs and Immigration Officers (ie border control).

The driver may encounter any one or more of these officials in the course of his or her work.

Disciplinary Powers of Traffic Commissioners

Traffic Commissioners retain disciplinary powers over PSV drivers. Schedule 2 of the **Road Traffic (Driver Licensing and Information Systems) Act 1989** allows for the referral by the Secretary of State for Transport of questions relating to the conduct of applicants for, or holders of, the PCV entitlement to the Traffic Commissioner, and where the Commissioner notifies the Secretary of State that the applicant or holder is not in his or her opinion a fit person to hold the entitlement, the Secretary of State must refuse to grant a licence, revoke or suspend the licence or disqualify the holder indefinitely or for a determined period.

Appeals against the refusal of the Secretary of State to reconsider refusing an applicant a licence, revoking or suspending a PCV entitlement or disqualifying a PCV driver can still be made to a magistrates' court (sheriff court in Scotland), and any Traffic Commissioner to whom the matter was referred then becomes the respondent in the case. PCV drivers must declare all convictions to their local Traffic Area Office.

A Traffic Commissioner may also determine that a driver may only drive a PCV as a provisional category D licence-holder until he or she passes a category D re-test.

Besides the considerable powers the Traffic Commissioners have, as described above, drivers should be aware of the powers of VOSA enforcement officers who may stop and inspect vehicles on the road and in transport premises, drive vehicles if necessary, issue prohibition notices and immobilise and/or impound vehicles where appropriate (*see also* pp.87–89).

Offences

A person who drives a PCV on the road without being in possession of the appropriate driving entitlement commits an offence. Also an employer that employs such a person for this purpose can be prosecuted. In both cases a fine on summary conviction can be imposed.

Endorsement and Disqualification

A disqualification by the courts from holding a category B entitlement will automatically disqualify the holder from driving a category D or D1 vehicle.

A PCV driver disqualified from holding a D or D1 entitlement will not automatically be debarred from holding a category B entitlement.

Unified driving licences (the photocard part of the current licence) do not contain statements of provisional driving licence entitlements or particulars of convictions, penalty points, endorsements and disqualifications — these are entered on a separate document (the green one) issued with the licence and known as the counterpart.

Duration

Currently category D and D1 entitlements are normally valid until age 45, or for five years if newly issued to someone over 40.

Renewals thereafter are every five years up to age 65, and then annually.

Medical reports are required at each renewal.

Maintenance Staff

Staff who have held a category C driving entitlement for at least two years may drive a category D vehicle in the following circumstances.

- The vehicle is damaged or is defective and is being driven to a place for repairs.
- The vehicle is being road tested after having been repaired.

The vehicle must not carry people who have no connection with the operator.

Holders of full category D licences may drive a PCV recovery vehicle (not articulated) up to 10.2 tonnes unladen weight.

Preserved Buses

Preserved or historic buses, defined as buses more than 30 years old, may be driven by the holder of a category B licence provided he or she is aged 21 or over, the vehicle is not carrying more than eight passengers and it is not being used for hire or reward.

4 CONDITION OF VEHICLES

CONSTRUCTION AND USE REGULATIONS

The **Motor Vehicles (Construction and Use) Regulations 1986** (SI 1986 No. 1078) as amended apply to all motor vehicles, both goods and passenger, as do the alternative EU regulations (2001/85/EC). Different types of vehicle are defined in the regulations, as listed below.

Definitions

Motor vehicle
A mechanically propelled vehicle intended or adapted for use on the roads.

Motor car and heavy motor car
A motor car is a mechanically propelled vehicle (excluding a motorcycle or invalid carriage) constructed to carry a load or passengers.

If the vehicle is a passenger vehicle it will be classed as a motor car if its unladen weight does not exceed 3050kg and it is adapted to carry not more than seven passengers.

A heavy motor car is a vehicle constructed to carry a load or up to eight passengers and exceeds 2540kg unladen weight.

Bus
A motor vehicle constructed or adapted to carry more than eight seated passengers in addition to the driver.

Articulated bus
A bus so constructed that it can be divided (but only by using workshop facilities) into two vehicles, one of which is a motor vehicle and passengers can at all times pass from one part to another.

Large bus
A vehicle constructed or adapted to carry 17 or more seated passengers in addition to the driver.

Coach
A large bus with a maximum gross weight of more than 7.5 tonnes and a maximum speed exceeding 60mph.

Minibus
A motor vehicle constructed or adapted to carry more than 8 but not more than 16 seated passengers.

Trailer
A vehicle drawn by a motor vehicle but excluding any part of an articulated bus.

Close-coupled
In relation to a trailer this means that the wheels on each side remain parallel to the longitudinal axis of the trailer when in motion and the centre of their respective areas of contact with the road does not exceed 1m.

Dual-purpose vehicle
A vehicle constructed or adapted for the carriage both of passengers and of goods or burden of any description, with an unladen weight not exceeding 2040kg and that either is capable of all-wheel drive or meets the following requirements as to body construction.

- It must have a permanently fitted rigid roof, with or without a sliding panel.
- The area to the rear of the driver's seat must:
  - be permanently fitted with at least one row of upholstered transverse seats (fixed or folding) for two or more passengers, and
  - have windows, of either glass or other transparent material, at the side and rear. The area or aggregate area of light on each side must be not less than $1850cm^2$ and at the rear not less than $770cm^2$.
- The distance between the rearmost part of the steering wheel and the back rests of the row of transverse seats

satisfying the requirements specified above (or, if there is more than one such row of seats, the distance to the rearmost such row) must, when the seats are ready for use, be not less than one-third of the distance between the rearmost part of the steering wheel and the rearmost part of the floor of the vehicle.

First used

Any provision applicable to a motor vehicle first used on or after a specified date need not apply to that vehicle if it was manufactured at least six months before the date.

Maximum Laden Weights

The maximum authorised weight of a loaded bus with two axles is 18 tonnes (18,000kg). The maximum authorised weight for a bus with three axles is 25,000kg and 30,000kg with four axles (26,000kg and 32,000kg respectively if fitted with "road friendly suspension", eg air suspension). Articulated buses may gross 28,000kg. These weights are as measured on the road and include water, oil, fuel, driver, passengers and luggage. The maximum drive axle weight is 11,500kg. Some vehicles, particularly smaller ones, have lower design weights than these authorised maximum values.

It is most important that a vehicle does not exceed any of its maximum gross or axle weights shown on the manufacturer's plate. If it does, it is an absolute offence which will attract a fixed penalty and licence (penalty points) endorsements for the driver. If the enforcement authorities (VOSA) find a vehicle on the road overweight a prosecution will almost always follow and this can result in both the driver and the operator being heavily fined and being called to appear before the Traffic Commissioners.

The problems of overweight can occur in a number of ways, eg badly stowed luggage, passengers on trips to the continent taking advantage of lower priced goods such as wines, beers and spirits and "stocking up" before making the return trip, etc.

While the operator should advise passengers of the constraints on the amount of baggage they can carry, the driver should also remind them of these limits, especially in the second example given above, as any surplus may have to be jettisoned if the police or an examiner from VOSA decide to check-weigh the vehicle. If the coach is found overweight the police or enforcement officer will require the excess to be offloaded before allowing it to proceed.

Maximum Dimensions for Buses and Coaches

The designs of PSVs are progressively reflecting the differing operational requirements between luxury or commuter coaches and scheduled and registered bus services, recognising the public's desire for greater accessibility in such vehicles. Either UK or EU regulations can be used to meet the needs of the vehicle operator and its passengers.

The overall maximum length for a non-articulated bus is 13.5m on two axles and 15m on three or more axles. A bus towing a trailer or an articulated bus must not exceed 18.75m.

Maximum height is 4.57m, but is limited to 4m when going to the Continent. Maximum width is 2.55m (excluding any guide wheels, which may project 75mm).

Manufacturer's Plates

All buses, including articulated buses, except those first used before 1 April 1982, must be fitted with a manufacturer's plate containing the:

- manufacturer's name
- vehicle type
- engine type and power
- chassis or serial number
- number of axles
- maximum axle weight for each axle
- maximum gross weight
- maximum train weight
- maximum weight in Great Britain for each axle
- maximum gross weight in Great Britain.

Twin Wheels

When vehicle axles are fitted with twin-tyred wheels or wide tyres ("big singles" in common terminology) their maximum permitted weights are as follows.

	Under C&U regulations (kg)	**Under authorised weight regulations (kg)**
Single non-driven axle	10,170	10,000
Single driving axle	10,500	11,500

Note: Under the Construction and Use (C&U) Regulations twin-wheel/tyre assemblies must have their centres of contact with the road surface at least 300mm apart. Wide tyres must be at least 300mm wide.

Speedometers

These must be fitted to all motor vehicles registered from 1 October 1937. Requirements for accuracy apply to speedometers incorporated in analogue type tachographs, which are required to operate within specified tolerances.

Vehicles first used from 1 April 1984 must be fitted with an instrument which allows the speed indication to be read in both mph and kph either simultaneously or by the operation of a separate switch.

Vehicles limited by either law or their construction to a speed not exceeding 25mph do not require speedometers.

Speedometers must be maintained in good working order at all "material times", ie when a vehicle is used on a journey unless:

- a defect occurs during a journey, or
- following a defect, steps are taken to have the equipment repaired or replaced as soon as possible.

Drivers should report any vehicle where the speedometer is:

- not fitted

- inoperative
- not illuminated
- not visible to the driver, or
- affected by a broken or missing dial glass.

The requirement to fit speedometers does not extend to vehicles fitted with EC-approved analogue tachograph recording equipment, as such instruments include speedometers.

Speed Limiters

Every coach exceeding a gross vehicle weight of 7.5 tonnes first used between 1 April 1974 and 31 December 1987 must be fitted with a speed limiter if it would otherwise be capable of exceeding 70mph. The limiter for these vehicles must be set at or below 70mph.

Buses and coaches first used between 1 January 1988 and 1 January 2005, with a maximum gross weight exceeding 10.0 tonnes and capable of a speed exceeding 100kph must be fitted with a speed limiter calibrated to a set speed not exceeding 100kph.

Buses and coaches first used between 1 October 2001 and 31 December 2004, with a maximum gross vehicle weight between 7.5 tonnes and 10.0 tonnes and capable of a speed exceeding 100kph, must be fitted with a speed limiter calibrated to enable a stabilised speed not exceeding 100kph.

Since 1 January 2005 all new buses and coaches, irrespective of weight or type of fuel, must be fitted with a speed limiter enabling a stabilised speed not exceeding 100kph.

Speed limiters must be sealed to prevent their being tampered with and the vehicle must display a plate in a conspicuous position in the driving compartment clearly marked with the set speed.

Tachographs

In accordance with EU regulations, tachographs must be fitted to all vehicles adapted or constructed for the commercial carriage of more than nine persons, including the driver. Such vehicles first registered after 1 May 2006 must be fitted with a digital tachograph. (For more detailed information on tachographs, see *The Tachograph*, pp.115–128.)

Warning Devices

Buses and coaches having an overall travelling height exceeding 3m must have either:

- a notice displayed in a prominent position in the driving compartment showing the overall travelling height of the vehicle, or
- documents such as a map, or maps, within easy reach of the driver giving details of the route, or choice of routes which can be taken, to eliminate the risk of the vehicle striking bridges or other overhead structures during the course of the journey.

If the former is adopted the notice must show the overall travelling height in feet and inches, or both in feet and inches and in metres; the numbers used for giving the height in feet and inches must be at least 40mm tall and those giving this information in feet and inches and metres must not differ by more than 50mm.

The total height shown in the notice must be not less than the travelling height of the vehicle nor more than 150mm above that height.

Television Sets

Television-receiving apparatus may not be installed in a motor vehicle if the screen is partly or wholly visible to the driver (either directly or reflected) while driving the vehicle, unless it is only capable of displaying information:

- about the state of the vehicle or its equipment
- about the location of the vehicle on the road
- to assist the driver in seeing the road adjacent to the vehicle
- to enable the driver to monitor passenger safety at the centre entrance/exit doors
- to assist the driver in reaching the destination.

Note: The second and third points taken together effectively legalise closed-circuit TV reversing monitors.

Receiving monitors and videos
"Television-receiving apparatus" means a screen or monitor on which can be displayed an image derived from a television broadcast, recording, camera or computer.

Performing rights
If recorded music or image equipment is to be played in a coach (either by radio, television or video), licences must be obtained by the operator. Details are available from the relevant bodies, as follows:

- radio — PRS for Music, tel: 0845 309 3090, website: *www.prsformusic.com*
- audio (cassette or CD) — PPL, tel: 020 7534 1000, website: *www.ppluk.com*
- video or DVD — either by an umbrella licence for the vehicle or by renting specific films, which includes all royalties:
  - umbrella licences — MPLC, tel: 01323 649647, website: *www.themplc.co.uk*
  - film rental — Filmbank Distributors, tel: 020 7984 5950, website: *www.filmbank.co.uk*.

A scale of fees applies in respect of each coach with equipment installed (equipment can be transferred between coaches).

Mirrors

All passenger and dual-purpose vehicles must have at least three rear view mirrors, two fitted externally — one on the offside and the other on the nearside — and the third internally (unless a mirror so fitted would be inadequate) to show traffic to the rear and both sides rearwards. On all vehicles registered from 1 April 1969 the edges of the internal mirror must be covered by a protective material.

On all vehicles registered after 1 June 1978 both the offside mirror and internal mirror must be capable of adjustment from the driving seat.

Vehicles over 3.5 tonnes maximum gross weight must be fitted with "close-proximity" external mirrors giving a view of both rearward approaching and overtaking traffic.

Each exterior rear view mirror must be visible to the driver either through a side window or through the part of the windscreen swept by the wiper. Drivers should ensure that their mirrors are always clean and correctly positioned to give immediate viewing from the driving position.

All minibuses first used from 1 April 1988 must be fitted with rear view mirrors or other means (for example, where a rear door is used as a service door, a rear view lens) to enable a seated driver to see the area immediately outside a service door. This requirement is deemed to be met if a driver can see a child 1.3m high standing 1m behind his or her vehicle.

Safety Glass

Passenger and dual-purpose vehicles must have safety glass fitted to the windscreen and all windows on the outside of the vehicle.

The safety glass fitted to the windscreen and all windows wholly or partly in front of and on either side of the driver's seat of motor vehicles manufactured from 1 December 1977 and first used from 1 June 1978 must conform to specifications BS 857. The "safety glass" fitted to other windows of a bus (including minibuses) may be safety glazing provided that the windows do not:

- face the rear of the vehicle, and
- form the whole or part of a door giving access to the exterior of the vehicle.

Partitions (ie transverse glass windows or panels) not made of safety glass are permissible provided that they are adequately protected against the likelihood of breakage by passengers being thrown against them.

Safety glass for windows on the upper deck of buses is mandatory for vehicles manufactured on or after 1 October 1981.

Windscreens and windows should be kept clean to ensure a clear view of the road and other traffic.

Windscreen Wipers and Washers

An efficient automatic windscreen wiper or wipers must be fitted to every vehicle from which an adequate view to the front cannot be obtained other than through the windscreen.

Wipers must be capable of ensuring the driver an adequate view of the road to the front and the front of the near and offsides. Such vehicles, unless they are being used to provide a local service or on a journey incidental to such use, must also be fitted with a windscreen washer which, in conjunction with the wiper, can keep the screen clear of mud, etc.

Horns and Reversing Alarms

Every motor vehicle must be fitted with an instrument capable of giving audible and sufficient warning of its approach or position. Only a vehicle used on official emergency services may be fitted with a gong, bell siren, two-tone horn or instrument capable of emitting a similar sound.

A reversing alarm may be fitted to a bus, provided the sound emitted by the alarm is different to that which is employed at "pelican" pedestrian crossings.

Reversing alarms and horns may not be sounded when the vehicle is stationary on a road nor when it is in motion on a restricted road at night between the hours of 2330 and 0700, except in an emergency. Horns may be sounded on a stationary vehicle:

- to warn of the presence to or of another moving vehicle on or near the road
- to raise the alarm as to theft of the vehicle or its contents
- on a bus to summon assistance for the driver, conductor or inspector.

Fuel Tanks

Motor vehicle fuel tanks must be so maintained that they are reasonably secure against damage and are free from leakages. Motor vehicles first used from 1 July 1973 must be equipped with metal fuel tanks but this requirement does not apply where the vehicle is legibly and indelibly marked with a designated approval mark indicating that the vehicle has been approved in respect of fire risks.

Smoke and Emissions

Every motor vehicle must be so constructed that no avoidable smoke or visible vapour is emitted.

It is an offence to drive a vehicle which is emitting smoke or dangerous vapour.

Specific European exhaust emissions standards have progressively applied to buses and coaches first registered on or after:

1 October 1993	EURO-I
1 October 1996	EURO-II
1 October 2001	EURO-III
1 October 2006	EURO-IV
1 October 2009	EURO-V

EURO-VI will apply to buses and coaches first registered on or after 1 January 2014.

Vehicles adapted to qualify for the higher standards, by having equipment such as a particulate trap fitted to prevent the emission of solid matter, may allow an operator to claim a Reduced Pollution Certificate for the vehicle — enabling payment reduction on Vehicle Excise Duty.

Low Emission Zones (LEZ)

Local authorities have powers to impose minimum EURO emission standards on vehicles entering a defined area and to make charges on vehicles which do not meet the set minimum standard.

Greater London was the first authority to introduce an LEZ, for buses and coaches from July 2008 and for minibuses from 2012. More than 70 UK towns and cities and many places abroad now have Low Emission or Environmental Zones in force.

Tyres

It is illegal to use on a vehicle a tyre:

(a) that is not correctly inflated
(b) that has a break in its fabric or a cut in excess of 25mm or 10% of the section width of the tyre, deep enough to reach the body cords
(c) that has a lump, bulge or tear caused by separation, etc
(d) that is the wrong size or type for the vehicle's use
(e) that has any portion of ply or cord exposed
(f) on which the base of any groove that showed in the original tread pattern is not clearly visible
(g) on which either:
    (i) the grooves of the tread pattern do not have a depth of at least 1mm throughout a continuous band measuring at least three quarters of the breadth of tread and round the entire outer circumference of the tyre, or
    (ii) where the original tread pattern did not extend beyond three quarters of the breadth of the tread, the base of any groove which showed in the tyre's original tread pattern does not have a depth of at least 1mm.

Note: The grooves of the tread pattern of tyres fitted to passenger vehicles with up to nine seats, goods vehicles not exceeding 3500kg maximum gross weight and light trailers must be a minimum of 1.6mm in depth throughout a continuous band situated in the central three quarters of the breadth of tread and round the entire outer circumference of the tyre.

"Breadth of tread" means the breadth of that part of the tyre which is in contact with the road under normal conditions of use measured at 90° to the peripheral line of the tread. "Tread pattern" means the combination of plain surfaces and grooves extending across the breadth of the tread and round the entire outer circumference of the tyres excluding:

- any tie-bars or tread wear indicators
- any features which are designed to wear out substantially before the rest of the pattern under normal conditions of use, and
- any other minor features.

"Tie-bars" means any part of the tyre moulded in the tread pattern of the tyre for the purpose of bracing two or more features of such tread pattern.

"Tread wear indicators" means any bar, not being a tie-bar, projecting from the base of the tread pattern and moulded between two or more features of the tyre's tread pattern for the purpose of indicating the extent of wear of such a tread pattern.

Points (a), (b) and (e) above do not apply where the tyre and wheel to which it is fitted are so constructed that when running deflated the tyre will operate safely and its outside wall bears an identifying mark to that effect.

These regulations do not apply to a broken-down vehicle or a vehicle being taken to a place to be broken up where in either case it is being towed by a vehicle not exceeding 20mph.

Recut pneumatic tyres must not be used if the ply or cord has been cut or exposed by the recutting process or it has been wholly or partially recut in a different pattern to that of the manufacturer's recut tread pattern.

It is also illegal to fit to motor vehicles having only two axles and equipped with one or two single wheels, tyres of different types, ie cross-ply, radial or bias-belted, in combinations of:

- diagonal-ply tyres or bias-belted tyres on the rear axle and radial-ply tyres on the front axle, or

- diagonal-ply tyres on the rear axle and bias-belted tyres on the front axle.

This does not apply if wide tyres, other than those used for engineering plant, are fitted.

Also, tyres of different structures must not be fitted to vehicles with:

- more than one steerable axle, or
- more than one driven axle not being a steerable axle.

Maintenance of tyres

Although maintenance of tyres, like total vehicle maintenance, is the responsibility of the maintenance staff, there are certain periodical checks that are the responsibility of the driver.

The following daily checklist is therefore recommended.

- Check tyre pressures (cold). Tyres generate heat during running and more so during hot weather, which may cause pressures to rise some 10–15 pounds above the recommended pressure.
- Examine tyres for cuts, blisters and stones, etc especially between twin tyres. At first sight these may not appear to be dangerous, but they may become so in the course of a journey.
- Check twin rear tyres. Inner and outer tyres should have the same diameter and the same pressure. One twin tyre below pressure will cause overloading of the other and an eventual blow-out.
- Make sure that all tyres show a reasonable amount of tread pattern and that the spare wheel and tyre are in similar good order and inflated to the correct pressure.

Tyre service and supply

For the benefit of operators or owner-drivers, the tyre manufacturers and their distributors offer substantial repair and replacement facilities.

Check the *Yellow Pages* or other sources for your nearest supplier.

Tyre loads and speed ratings

Vehicles must be fitted with tyres designed to support their maximum axle weights when driven at the maximum legal speed limits.

Doors

It is an offence to open the door of a vehicle when the vehicle is moving or when this may cause injury or damage to any person.

Seat Belts and Anchorage Points

The exact requirement for seat belts and anchorage points depends on the type of vehicle, its weight and date of first use. Generally all cars, passenger or dual-purpose vehicles constructed to carry 12 or fewer people (excluding the driver), minibuses under 3500kg, and certain light goods vehicles under 3500kg must be provided with seat belts and anchorage points for the driver's seat and front passenger seats (either all seats or a "specified" seat, eg the one next to the driver).

This "basic" requirement was extended to all "exposed" forward-facing seats of coaches first used on or after 1 October 1988, and still further in 2001 when seat belts were required at all forward and rearward-facing seats of all non-urban buses first used on or after 1 October 2001. These fitting requirements are independent of the use requirement for minibuses and coaches carrying children (see later).

The fitting of seats with integral seat belts, anchorage points and built-in seat belts is allowed as an alternative to conventional seat belt anchorage points and seat belts.

Some vehicle types first used from 1 April 1973 must be fitted with seat belts which can be put on with one hand and which must be easy to adjust and stow away. The stowing device must prevent the belt from lying on the floor.

Seat belts and anchorage points must be maintained in a proper condition at all times so that the belt, its anchorages, fastenings and adjusting device are free from any obvious defects which would seriously affect the proper functioning of the seat belt in the event of an accident. Anchorage points and all load-bearing parts of the vehicle's structure or panelling within 30cm of each anchorage point must at all times be free from serious corrosion, distortion or fracture.

All passenger vehicles with nine or fewer seats, including the driver's, must have seat belt anchorage points which comply with EU requirements for every forward-facing seat. The same EU standard applies to all anchorage points fitted after 1 October 2001.

Rear seat belts

Cars and dual-purpose vehicles first used on or after 1 January 1987 must be fitted with rear seat belts as follows.

- Vehicles with not more than two forward-facing seats behind the driver's seat require:
  - an inertia reel belt for at least one seat, or
  - a three-point, lap, or disabled person's belt or child restraint for each seat.
- Vehicles with more than two (ie up to six) forward-facing seats behind the driver's seat require:
  - an inertia reel belt for one outboard seat and a three-point, lap or disabled person's belt for at least one other seat, or
  - a three-point belt for one seat and either a child restraint or disabled person's belt for at least one other seat (one of the two seats fitted must be an outboard seat), or
  - a three-point, lap or disabled person's belt or child restraint for each of those seats.

Seat Belts on Buses Carrying Children

Seat belts are required to be fitted to forward-facing seats in minibuses and coaches carrying all children (not just school children) aged under 16 whenever a group of three or more children is on an "organised trip" and where the journey is made for the purpose of the trip, ie it is used specifically where the transport of children is central to the purpose of the journey.

The regulations *do not* apply where the children are travelling on a vehicle used to provide a registered service (so long as it is not an excursion or tour), or a service provided under a London Local Service Permit or on behalf of TfL, where 50% or more of the seats are available to the general public, or services used "wholly or mainly to provide a transport service for the general public", even if these incidentally allow some child passengers to make an "organised trip" as defined above.

3 for 2 concession
The concession under which three seated children of 14 or under count as two children for the purpose of carrying capacity is qualified so that it only applies if none is occupying a seat fitted with a belt.

Wearing of Seat Belts

Drivers and front seat passengers (ie those seated alongside the driver) of all vehicles must wear the seat belts provided.

Exemptions from these requirements are given for specific people, including:

- the driver when reversing a vehicle
- a driving instructor (as defined in the driving licences regulations) while supervising a learner driver in a manoeuvre that includes reversing
- the holder of a certificate signed by a registered medical practitioner, exempting him or her from wearing seat belts, on medical grounds
- a qualified tester who is conducting a person in a driving test and who, by wearing a seat belt, would endanger him or herself or any other person
- a person occupying a seat where the seat belt either does not conform to the C&U Regulations, or has an inertia reel mechanism which is locked because the vehicle is on, or has been on, a steep incline
- a person riding in a vehicle under trade plates while investigating or remedying a mechanical fault in the vehicle

- a constable protecting or escorting another person
- a prison officer protecting or escorting another person
- firemen
- a taxi driver while seeking hire, answering a call for hire, or carrying a passenger for hire, or the driver of a private hire vehicle while the vehicle is being used to carry a passenger for hire.

It is the responsibility of the individual to wear the seat belt but responsibility rests with the driver when a child under the age of 14 is being carried in the front seat of any vehicle with a gvw of less than 3.5 tonnes.

Children under the age of 14 carried in the rear seat of any motor car (excluding a taxi) must wear any "available" seat belts.

Fines can be imposed where these regulations are not complied with.

There is no lower age limit for these regulations but if the passenger is under 14 he or she will not be allowed in the middle front passenger seat without an approved seat belt (it is illegal to carry an unrestrained child in the front seat of virtually any vehicle). Children over one year old may use an adult seat belt or other approved device, unless they are disabled, when they may use any specially designed and constructed seat belt. Disabled adults must use a standard seat belt unless they are in a specially constructed or adapted vehicle, when they may use any seat belt specially designed for them.

Trailers

Maximum laden weights

For trailers manufactured from 27 February 1977 with brakes that operate automatically on overrun and irrespective of any other brakes, the maximum laden weight is 3500kg. The laden weight of an unbraked trailer used on the road must not exceed its maximum gross weight. It may only be towed by a vehicle whose kerbside weight is at least double the unladen weight of the trailer together with the weight of any load the trailer is carrying. Trailers under 750kg gross weight must be fitted with brakes if their laden weight exceeds half the towing vehicle's weight.

Unbraked trailers (markings)
Every unbraked trailer must be marked in a conspicuous and readily accessible position on the left or nearside with its maximum gross weight (in kg).

Detached trailers
When detached from the drawing vehicle a trailer must be prevented from moving by the use of a brake, chain, chock or other efficient device applied to at least one of its wheels.

Length of tow rope
Where a motor vehicle is drawing a trailer by means of a tow rope or chain, the distance between their nearest points must not exceed 4.5m. Where the distance exceeds 1.5m the tow rope or chain must be made clearly visible from both sides. No limit of length is stated for a rigid tow bar.

Carriage of passengers in trailers
PSV (C&U) Regulations prohibit the use of trailers for the conveyance of passengers for hire or reward. Broken-down vehicles carrying passengers may be towed provided they are not drawn faster than 30mph and the vehicles are attached by a rigid draw bar.

PSVs drawing trailers
A bus or coach must not draw a trailer unless:
- it is an empty bus drawing another empty bus which has broken down, or
- it is a trailer and the overall length of the combination does not exceed 18.75m.

No trailer may, in any circumstances, be drawn by an articulated bus.

Vehicles with rear exits are prohibited from drawing any trailers. While passengers are being carried by a vehicle no person must cause or permit any unnecessary obstruction to any entrance, exit or gangway of the vehicle.

This means that if the vehicle has a rear exit a trailer *must not* be attached.

Passengers must not be carried in a trailer used for hire or reward unless it is a broken-down bus towed at a speed less than 30mph by a rigid draw bar.

Note: The small motorised "road trains" often used in tourist areas are not PSVs; they are subject to special rules.

Brakes

The C&U Regulations lay down specific requirements for the design, application and maintenance of brakes. They do so, in most cases, by applying the requirements of Directive 79/489/EC (as amended).

Every passenger vehicle and trailer (except small trailers with total axle weights not exceeding 750kg) first used on or after 1 April 1983 must comply with the EC Directive. Vehicles first used before that date may also comply with the Directive or may comply with the C&U Regulations.

Parking brake

Every passenger vehicle must have a parking brake that is independent of the main brakes and capable, by direct mechanical action, of holding the vehicle stationary on a gradient of at least 16% (ie 1 in 6.25). If the vehicle is required to meet EU braking standards its parking brake must be capable of holding it with an *unbraked* trailer attached on a gradient of 12% (1 in 8.33). A spring brake can be considered to be a mechanical means of action.

Main and secondary brakes

Every passenger vehicle's braking system must have a main means of operation (ie the footbrake) and a secondary means, which could be an emergency brake or a dual system, the "split" part of which is also operated by the footbrake. If one half of the braking system fails, the remainder must continue to operate with the required residual efficiency. In the case of a vehicle with a dual braking system, the parking brake must be able to operate with the vehicle in motion unless it is a transmission brake.

Retarders

Use may be made of a retarder to assist a vehicle to comply with EU braking specifications on downhill speed control and brake fade, but no account may be taken of the contribution of the retarder to assist in complying with the braking efficiencies referred to below.

Anti-lock Braking System (ABS)

A coach over 12t gross weight first used on or after 1 April 1992 must be equipped with a category 1 (individual wheel) anti-lock brake system. This requirement extends to new buses first used on or after 1 May 2002.

A vehicle developing a failure in its ABS may be driven to complete its journey and/or to a place of repair *provided* the brakes otherwise comply with the C&U Regulations.

Braking efficiences

The general minimum braking efficiencies for vehicles to which the regulations apply are as follows:

	Minimum braking efficiencies (%)		
	Parking brake	**Main brake**	**Second-ary brake**
Passenger vehicles complying with the EC directive and first used on or after 1 April 1983	16	50	25
If drawing a trailer	12	45	25

Application of trailer brakes

The driver must be able to operate the brakes of both the motor vehicle and its trailer, except where the trailer is fitted with an overrun brake, or the trailer is a broken-down vehicle being towed in such a manner that it cannot be steered by its own steering gear.

Turning Circles (Swept Circle) and Cut Out

All buses registered in the UK since 9 March 2005 have had to meet the turning circle requirements as set out in Directive 96/53/EC (as amended by Directive 2002/7/EC) instead of the previously applicable UK C&U Regulations (see diagrams below).

Turning Circle

Turning Circle
The vehicle has to manoeuvre between 2 concentric circles of 12.5 metres and 5.3 metres radius

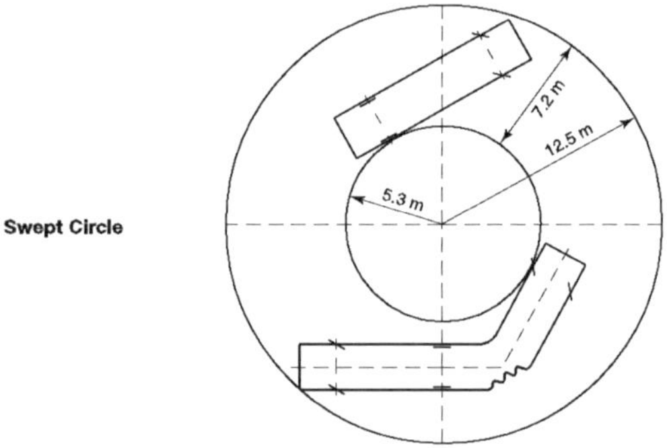

Cut out (out-swing)

When moving forward from a straight line position where the nearside front corner of the vehicle is positioned on the outer of the two circles shown in the diagram below, to turn in a clockwise direction, no part of the vehicle shall move outside of the vertical plane by more than 0.6m. (See diagram on the next page.)

Cut Out (Out-swing)

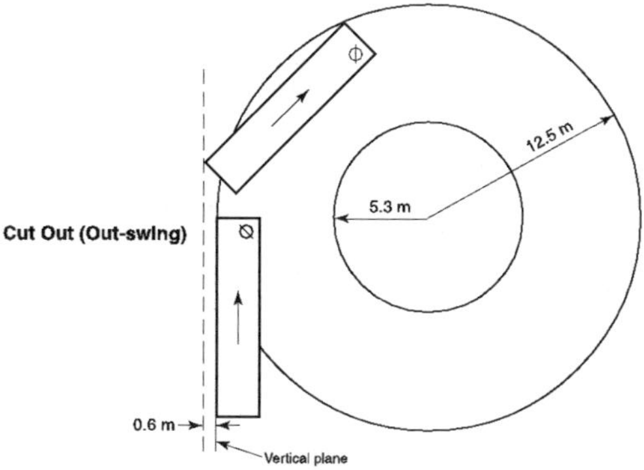

Reproduced with the kind permission of VOSA.

Articulated Buses

The test is the same for articulated vehicles except that the two rigid portions of the vehicle must be aligned with the vertical plane before moving in the clockwise direction.

Roof Strength of Coaches

All single-deck "high floor" (ie with below-deck luggage lockers) coaches first used on or after 1 April 1993 must comply with ECE (Economic Commission for Europe) Regulation 66 requiring sufficient roof strength to provide a passenger survival space in a "roll-over" accident.

Noise

No motor vehicle or trailer which causes excessive noise may be used on the road, nor may it be used in a manner to cause excessive noise which could be avoided.

Noise or excessive noise emitted by a vehicle includes that emitted by an inefficient exhaust silencer.

LIGHTING

Between sunset and sunrise (and during periods of seriously reduced visibility) all vehicles are required to carry two front lamps showing white to the front, two rear position lamps showing red to the rear, two red "retro" reflectors, a rear registration plate lamp and end outline marker lamps (if applicable). Buses also require two headlamps.

Restrictions

- A red light must not be shown to the front of a vehicle.
- A white light must not be shown to the rear of a vehicle except:
  - for the purpose of reversing
  - in order to illuminate the interior of a vehicle
  - to illuminate the rear number plate
  - to illuminate a PSV destination board or a taxi meter.

Special provisions do permit the use of blue, amber or green lights on fire, ambulance, or police service vehicles, medical practitioners' vehicles and special service vehicles.

Use of headlamps and auxiliary lamps

Headlamps must be used during the hours of darkness in all unlit areas (or where the street lamps are more than 200 yards apart). "Hours of darkness" is usually defined as half an hour after sunset to half an hour before sunrise.

Both lights must be illuminated together and it is an offence to drive in non-illuminated areas (where street lamps are more than 200 yards apart) with only one headlamp working.

Headlamps must be switched off when the vehicle is stationary except at traffic stops. They must not be fitted more than 1200mm from the ground, nor less than 500mm from the ground.

Headlamps must be fitted with a dipping mechanism to avoid dazzle and no light other than a dipping headlamp may be moved, by swivelling or otherwise, while the vehicle is in motion. Every matched pair of headlamps must emit beams of the same colour light. Lamps fitted and used as fog or spotlights must be fitted with a permanently deflected beam. There is no minimum height for these lamps provided they are used only during poor visibility.

A vehicle being towed and a snow plough are exempt from using headlamps.

Front Fog Lamps

In conditions where visibility is seriously reduced, two fog lamps or a fog lamp and a spot lamp may be used instead of headlamps.

Fog lamps may emit either a white or yellow light and must be positioned so that they do not dazzle or cause inconvenience to other road users.

High Intensity Rear Fog Lamps

Rear fog lamps must be fitted to vehicles and trailers first used from 1 April 1980. Either a single or a matched pair of rear fog lamps can be fitted.

Rear fog lamps may only be used in conditions of poor visibility and must be switched off as soon as conditions improve. They must not be wired through to the vehicle brake light circuit.

Direction Indicators

All vehicles must be fitted with direction indicators of the flashing type. Indicators on vehicles first used from September 1965 must show amber both to the front and rear. They must flash at a rate of between 60 and 120 flashes per minute.

Emergency Service Vehicles

Distinctive lamps emitting blue, amber or green flashing lights are permitted on certain vehicles carrying out emergency or other services.

Ambulances, fire engines, fire salvage vehicles, Forestry Commission or local authority vehicles used for fire-fighting, police vehicles, HM Revenue and Customs, blood transfusion service vehicles, bomb disposal, Royal Air Force mountain rescue vehicles, HM Coastguard or coastguard auxiliary vehicles used for emergencies on or near the coast, Mines Rescue Service vehicles, Royal National Lifeboat Institution vehicles used for launching lifeboats and vehicles used for carrying human tissue for transplants, etc are permitted to carry one or more *blue* lamps.

Vehicles used for road clearance; for testing, maintaining, improving, cleansing or watering roads; inspecting, renewing or installing any apparatus in, on, under or over a road; vehicles constructed or adapted for refuse collection; vehicles having a maximum speed not exceeding 25mph; vehicles having an overall width exceeding 2.9m; breakdown vehicles; vehicles authorised by an Order under s.44 of the **Road Traffic Act 1988**, ie special type vehicles or trailers constructed for special purposes, etc are permitted to carry one or more *amber* lights.

Highways Agency Traffic Officer vehicles carry amber, white and rear-red flashing lights.

Vehicles used by registered medical practitioners registered by the General Medical Council may carry one or more *green* lamps when used in an emergency.

Warning beacons fitted to vehicles used to escort wide loads at speeds in excess of 25mph and vehicles used at airports may emit a *yellow* light.

All such lamps must be fitted so that the centre is at least 1200mm above the ground and be visible from any point at a reasonable distance from the vehicle. The frequency of the flashing from these lamps must not be less than 60 nor more than 240 equal times per minute and the interval between each flashing must be constant.

The lamps may only be used when the vehicle is being used for the relevant purposes and in the case of a breakdown vehicle the amber lights may only be illuminated when the vehicle is being used in connection with, or near to, an accident or breakdown, or towing a disabled vehicle. Such vehicles are permitted an additional white lamp for illuminating the area of the accident or breakdown but it must be directed so as not to dazzle or inconvenience other road users.

Road clearance vehicles are also permitted to carry an amber reflecting surface to the rear of the vehicle.

Stop Lights, Reversing Lights and Trailer Lights

Stop lights must be fitted to all vehicles and must always be maintained in a clean and efficient working order.

Reversing lights are not compulsory fittings but if fitted to a vehicle they must be maintained in efficient working order.

Use of Hazard Warning Lights

Hazard warning lights may be used only when the vehicle is stationary on any part of the road, for the purpose of warning other drivers that the vehicle is temporarily causing an obstruction or while travelling on motorways or unrestricted dual carriageways to warn drivers of following vehicles of the need to slow down because of an obstruction ahead. They may also be used by drivers of buses to summon assistance for the driver, conductor or an inspector on the bus, or while a bus displaying "school bus" signs is embarking or disembarking children.

Lights Required During Daylight Hours

With effect from 7 August 2012, new vehicles may only be approved for initial use if they are fitted with daytime running lights.

The law also requires vehicles travelling on a road where visibility is seriously reduced to have obligatory lamps switched on, ie side and rear position lamps and either headlamps or a pair of front fog lamps and rear fog lamps.

It should be noted that front and rear fog lamps may only be used in conditions where visibility is seriously reduced during the day or at night — it is illegal to use them at any other time.

Lights Required on Stationary Vehicles at Night

Passenger vehicles other than buses (ie with seats for more than eight passengers such as people carriers) may be parked at night on a restricted road (ie within a 30mph zone) *without lights* if:

- they are parked with their nearside close to and parallel to the kerb (except when standing in a recognised parking place or on either side of a one-way street), and
- no part of the vehicle is within 10m of a road junction.

No lights are required on a vehicle if it is parked within the confines of an area outlined by lamps or traffic signs (cones) to prevent the vehicle, etc from being a danger to other road users.

Any vehicle to which a trailer is attached must keep its lights (side lamps) on when parked on the road at night.

(See also *Parking on the Road at Night without Lights*, p.213.)

General Requirements

Headlamps, front and rear fog lamps and reversing lamps (if fitted) must be set so that they do not dazzle or cause inconvenience to other road users. It is also a requirement of the law that all lights and reflectors, including hazard warning lights, are kept clean and in good working order.

Number Plates

Vehicles, including trailers, not exceeding three tonnes unladen weight, first registered on or after 1 January 1973 must be fitted with reflex-reflecting number plates. Only the background may be made of retro-reflective material and this must be white for the front plate and yellow for the back plate with letters and figures in black on both.

Vehicles first registered before 1 January 1973 may also be fitted with reflex-reflecting number plates as an alternative to the earlier "white on black" number plates.

A trailer (including a broken-down vehicle being towed) must have the registration number of the towing vehicle fitted on the rear of the vehicle on tow.

Vehicles first registered on or after 1 September 2001 must be fitted with plates made of retro-reflecting material — with colour arrangements as above.

Nationality symbols may be shown on UK vehicle number plates (eg the Cross of St George for England, the Red Dragon for Wales and the Saltire for Scotland).

VEHICLE CERTIFICATION, APPROVAL, INSPECTION AND ANNUAL TESTING

While manufacturers and operators have the responsibility for the above, brief details are included in this guide since:

- owner-drivers will need the information, and
- employee-drivers should be aware of the requirements of the legislation and be able to check that the vehicles they drive comply.

Individual Vehicle Approval for New Buses

New buses or coaches registered on or after 29 October 2010 are not eligible for a Certificate of Initial Fitness (COIF) but are subject to the new approval regime of the EC Whole Vehicle Type Approval (ECWVTA).

This change affects anyone who:

- manufactures buses or coaches
- certifies new buses or coaches using COIF
- supplies new buses for hire and reward or private use
- imports new buses or coaches from outside the EU.

Certification of Initial Fitness

No PSV which is adapted to carry more than eight passengers may be used unless either:

- a certifying officer has issued a COIF, or
- a certificate has been issued by the DfT approving the vehicle as a type vehicle of a particular type and a certifying officer (if he or she is satisfied that the vehicle complies with prescribed conditions of fitness) has issued a Certificate of Conformity, or
- a type approval certificate has been issued.

Once in service PSVs must be tested annually on the anniversary of their first registration (not their COIF date). Recertification is no longer required but the vehicles are subject to a system of prohibition where necessary.

If a COIF or Certificate of Conformity is issued before registration it must be sent to the DfT so that the registration number of the vehicle can be noted and the certificate returned.

Vehicle Inspections

All motor vehicles, including PSVs, are subject to spot checks, either at the roadside or at an operator's premises.

Authorised police officers and certain VOSA examiners may, on production of their authority, test or inspect a vehicle on the road. A police officer in uniform may require a vehicle to stop on the road and some accredited VOSA enforcement officers (usually in marked "stoppage" vehicles) have the same powers. They wear a uniform similar to that of a police officer and must display a Community Accreditation badge; they also drive specially liveried VOSA vehicles. It is an offence to obstruct an authorised examiner, although drivers of motor vehicles that are *not PSVs* may request a deferred test, which may be refused by a police officer if it appears to him or her that:

- because of an accident involving the vehicle a test should be immediately conducted, or

- the vehicle is so defective that it ought not to be allowed to proceed without first being tested.

If an authorised examiner discovers a defect he or she may, in addition to instituting proceedings for a breach of C&U Regulations, serve a defect notice on the owner via the driver (if he or she is not the owner) of the vehicle requiring, within 28 days, a certificate from a PSV testing station "clearing" the defect.

A VOSA examiner may drive a vehicle in order to test it. An examiner or police officer in uniform may inspect any motor vehicle on premises provided the consent of the owner of the vehicle and/or premises is obtained, or 48 hours' notice of intended inspection is given (72 hours if notice is sent by recorded delivery).

Operator Compliance Risk Score

Passenger vehicle operators are assigned a rating (or score) under the Operator Compliance Risk Score (OCRS) scheme operated by VOSA, which enables enforcement officers to identify, on past experience and records, which vehicles are least likely to comply with legal requirements. Ratings or scores are allocated for two areas: vehicle roadworthiness (based on annual test results, fleet checks and roadside checks), and general traffic enforcement (based on non-mechanical issues such as licensing, hours and tachographs). VOSA examiners refer to the scores at the roadside, via a small Mobile Compliance Device (MCD) which is linked to the VOSA database, to identify which vehicles should be checked.

The OCRS system was revised with effect from 1 October 2012, with the ratings described above placing operators into risk bands according to points gained over a three-year rolling period. The use of predictive scores was abandoned with the new arrangements.

Inspection of PSVs

The rules relating to inspection of PSVs by authorised police officers or VOSA examiners are stricter than those given above. They may enter premises to conduct tests at any reasonable time, carry out roadside checks, and if necessary detain vehicles to do so. There is no provision to opt for a delayed test. Drivers must give reasonable assistance to authorised police officers and examiners. Vehicle examiners or police officers in uniform may direct a vehicle which is stationary on a road to be taken to any place not more than five miles distant for inspection purposes. Powers to conduct roadside checks (but not fleet inspections) extend to all buses with more than eight seats, even if these are not PSVs.

Following an inspection as above authorised police officers and vehicle examiners have similar, but not identical, powers to prohibit the use of the vehicle. Both may issue an immediate prohibition if they consider the vehicle unfit for service, but only a vehicle examiner may issue a delayed prohibition. Prohibitions relating to passenger vehicles cannot be removed until the vehicle has been inspected in accordance with the directions on the prohibition, which can specify a re-test at an official PSV Testing Station or at an operator's premises if tests are conducted there.

The imposition of a prohibition and the use of a vehicle in contravention of a prohibition can have serious consequences for an operator and may even jeopardise the PSV "O" licence. Drivers should immediately report any prohibition received to their employers.

The forms of prohibition in use by the police and VOSA are as follows.

PG9	Prohibition of driving a vehicle on the road (applicable to ALL vehicles)
PG9/A/B/C	Combined Refusal/Variation and Exemption
PG9A	Variation of terms of a PG9

PG9B	Permitting the movement of a prohibited vehicle to a place of repair under stated conditions
PG9C	Refusal to remove a prohibition
PG9D	Prohibition/variation defect continuation sheet
PG10	Removal of a prohibition
PGDN(35)	Defect notice (where the defect does not warrant prohibition)
TE160	Prohibition of the movement of a vehicle due to overloading

Any PG9 marked (S) means that in the opinion of the inspectors the defect is such as to show a significant failure in the system of planned maintenance and is viewed very seriously by the Traffic Commissioner. If the PG9 is marked (X) this indicates that the defect is not maintenance-related.

Drivers (or their employers) are also legally bound to report to the Traffic Commissioner any damage or accident to a PSV which might affect the safety of its operation.

Weighing of Buses and Coaches

Persons authorised by a Highway Authority officer, or a police constable authorised in writing by a police authority or by a chief officer of police, may require a person in charge of a bus or coach to allow it or any trailer drawn by it to be weighed or to proceed to a weighbridge for that purpose.

There is no provision for authorised persons to require the bus or coach to be unloaded to ascertain unladen weight.

If, when the vehicle is weighed, it appears to either an authorised person (ie a police constable) or vehicle examiner that the C&U limits as to the weight of the vehicle have been exceeded or that by reasons of excess overall weight or excess axle weight the driving of the vehicle would involve danger or injury to any person, any of the above authorised persons may serve a notice (TE160) in writing prohibiting the driving of the overweight vehicle on the road until:

- the weight has been reduced, and
- official notice has been given to the person in charge of the vehicle that it is permitted to proceed.

Removal of a prohibition may be withheld until the vehicle has been re-weighed and, for this purpose, the authorised persons or vehicle examiner may give a direction in writing requiring the removal of the vehicle to a specified place subject to any conditions in the direction. Driving the vehicle under such a direction while overweight will not be an offence.

If the vehicle has to be removed more than five miles and is found not to be overweight the operator may claim compensation.

Vehicle Testing

Tests of passenger vehicles, including most PSVs and taxis, are carried out annually after their first examination (which is usually conducted on or before the first anniversary of their registration).

The only exception to this rule is the three year Class IV MOT test which applies to passenger vehicles with eight or fewer passenger seats (including such vehicles used as a PSV unless they have a COIF). Also within the scope of the Class IV MOT test are passenger vehicles with more than 8 but fewer than 13 passenger seats, but these have to be tested annually after one year. Class IV tests are usually carried out by an authorised examiner (ie private garages franchised for this purpose by the DfT) but may also be carried out by designated councils (ie county or district councils authorised for this purpose by the DfT) or an Authorised Testing Facility (ATF).

Vehicles with more than 12 passenger seats, including works buses, minibuses used under a minibus permit and buses which may lawfully be used on a road without a COIF (ie Community Buses and LEA school buses), require Class V tests. This is similar to a car MOT test but must be carried out:

- at a DfT testing station, and

- by a designated council, or at an Authorised Testing Facility (ATF) which is authorised to test vehicles in this class.

Drivers of such vehicles should check that their proposed test location is permitted to test Class V vehicles. PSVs with more than 8 seats and having a COIF and large buses (designed to carry more than 16 passengers, excluding the driver) require a Class VI test which is conducted by a DfT vehicle examiner either at a VOSA testing station or at certain designated or ATF premises. This test is more rigorous and comprehensive than the Class IV or V MOT tests and covers every item specified in the *PSV Inspection Manual* (available from *www.gov.uk/vosa*).

Summary

As previously stated, tests of passenger vehicles including PSVs and taxis are carried out annually after their first examination which is usually on or before the first anniversary of their registration (but may in a few cases be on or before their third anniversary). They may be carried out by DfT vehicle examiners, examiners authorised by the DfT to inspect vehicles (eg VOSA examiners) or designated councils. Tests undertaken at ATFs (Authorised Testing Facilities) are carried out by VOSA examiners. The table below shows, by seating capacity, the class of test to which various vehicles are subject, and by whom they are to be examined.

Class	Non-PSVs	PSVs	First examination after	Examined by		
				DfT	Authorised examiner	Designated council
IV	8 or fewer seats*	8 or fewer seats	3 years		✓	✓
V	more than 8 but 12 or fewer seats*		1 year		✓	✓
	more than 12 seats* including work buses and "Permit" minibuses	PSVs which can be used without COIF, ie Community Buses, LEA school buses	1 year	✓	✓	✓
VI		PSVs with more than 8 seats* not in Class V	1 year	✓	✓	—

* Excluding the driver's seat.

5 FITNESS, EQUIPMENT AND USE OF PSVs AND MINIBUSES

PSV CONDITIONS OF FITNESS

The **Public Service Vehicles (Conditions of Fitness, Equipment, Use and Certification) Regulations 1981** (SI 1981 No. 257) as amended by SI 2008 No. 1458 in regard to test fees, are the major source of legislation covering the design of PSVs. More recently, the Bus Construction Directive 2001/85/EC has defined the necessary requirements for new vehicles. Similar regulations apply to minibuses with between 9 and 16 seats (excluding the driver's seat) used under ss.18–21 of the **Transport Act 1985** (Permit minibuses and Community Buses). These regulations place no less emphasis on safety but relax or omit many of the "comfort" requirements (eg seat spacing or headroom). Minibuses usually now comply with the criteria in Schedules 6 and 7 of the **Road Vehicles (Construction and Use) Regulations 1986** (SI 1986 No. 1078).

Many of the requirements of the regulations do not apply to vintage vehicles.

The main provisions of the **PSV (Conditions of Fitness Equipment Use and Certification) Regulations 1981** likely to be of interest to drivers are detailed below.

Stability

PSVs are "tilt tested" at their first test for a COIF. During the test the vehicle must not overturn before the surface on which it stands has reached the following angles from the horizontal.

- Single deck, fully laden — tilt angle 35°.

• Double deck, top deck fully laden — tilt angle 28°.
For the test the vehicles must be loaded as shown below with weights of 63.5kg (representing a load of average passengers, driver, and, if carried, conductor).

Drivers should take great care where luggage is stowed on roof racks. It is advisable to try and prevent large numbers of school children congregating on the top deck of double-deck vehicles if the lower saloon is unoccupied.

Tilt Testing of PSVs

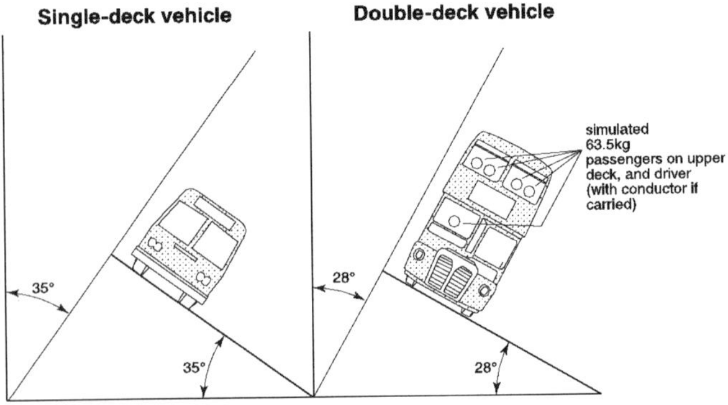

Guard rails or body "skirts" (if required due to a gap of more than 610mm between the wheels) between the front and rear wheels of a PSV must extend to within 310mm (12 inches approx) of the ground, 155mm (6 inches approx) from the rear wheel and 230mm (9 inches approx) from the front wheel when the vehicle is unladen, with no passengers and standing on level ground.

Brakes

The EU braking regulations now apply to:
• all passenger vehicles with eight or fewer seats

Guard Rails

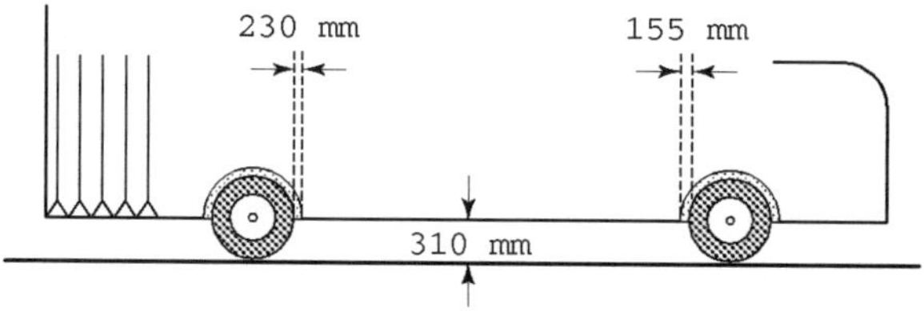

- buses first used before 1 April 1983 if they have a manufacturer's Certificate of Conformity certifying that they conform to EU regulations as a "type vehicle"
- buses first used after 1 April 1983.

There are additional requirements for PSVs that are not "type approved".

- All the brakes of a PSV must act directly on the wheels of the vehicle and not through the transmission.
- An exception is made for mechanically operated brakes which work without the intervention of any stored energy if:
  - there is no universal joint between the brake and the wheel
  - failure of any part of the mechanism would not cause the wheel to become detached, and
  - all the wheels of the vehicle are fitted with brakes operated by the same means.
- The brakes of one of the braking systems must be operated by a pedal.

Fuel Tanks

On lower decks of double-deck vehicles and single-deck vehicles with seats for more than 12 passengers, fuel tanks may not be positioned under gangways or within 600mm of a primary emergency exit, or anywhere in the driver or passenger compartments.

On single-deck passenger vehicles carrying not more than 12 passengers the fuel tank may not be placed under or within 300mm of any entrance or exit and the filling point must not be at the rear.

Fuel tanks must only be able to be filled from outside the vehicle.

There must be a fuel cut-off device accessible from outside the vehicle.

- On diesel-engined vehicles it need not be immediately visible so long as its position is clearly marked on the outside of the vehicle and the means of operation is clearly indicated.
- On petrol-engined vehicles it must be visible and the "off" position must be marked.

(Some smaller vehicles are fitted with dashboard-mounted emergency engine stops/fuel cut offs, often operated by means of the ignition key. Provided the key when turned to off stops the engine, and that the location and means of operation is correctly marked, this is not a reason for rejection when the vehicle is submitted for annual testing.)

The maintenance of fuel tanks is most important. Drivers should immediately report any insecure, leaking or corroded fuel tank or vehicles without a filler cap or with one of a type which does not prevent spillage.

Silencers and Noise

Every vehicle fitted with an internal combustion engine must be fitted with an exhaust system including a silencer. They must be maintained in good and efficient working order.

Exhaust gases must not escape into the atmosphere without first passing through the silencer fitted to the vehicle.

Vehicles are subject to spot checks on the road to ensure that they do not make more noise than the standards allow.

All vehicles registered after 1 April 1970 must meet stringent limits on noise. Newer vehicles are subject to even more stringent noise limits in so far as they relate to noise levels *measured on the road*. However, these do not apply to a vehicle proceeding to a place where by previous arrangement noise tests are to be carried out or adjustments, modifications or equipment are to be fitted so that the vehicle complies, or when a vehicle is returning from such a place immediately after the noise has been so tested.

Exhaust Pipes

Exhaust pipes must be so fitted or shielded so that there is no likelihood of any flammable material falling on them from any part of the vehicle and so that they are unlikely to cause a fire as a result of proximity to any flammable material on the vehicle.

The outlet should be either at the rear or offside and close enough to the rear to prevent, as far as possible, fumes entering the vehicle.

Drivers should report any exhaust system likely to create a fire or fume hazard, or which is wrongly positioned.

Outlets from ancillaries such as toilet, sink or cooking facilities must be designed to prevent the deposit of waste on the road surface.

Electrical Equipment

On vehicles registered on or after 19 June 1968 any electrical circuit with a voltage of over 100 volts must be capable of being isolated from the main supply by a dual pole switch readily accessible to the driver or conductor (unless one pole of the circuit is earthed).

The switch must not disconnect the obligatory lights required by the **Road Vehicles Lighting Regulations 1989**.

Body and Suspension

The body must be securely fixed to the chassis and every trap door or suspension flap secured so that it cannot become dislodged by vibration. Catches or lifting devices must not project above the floor.

The suspension must prevent any excessive body sway. Failure of any part of the suspension (except tyres) should not cause the driver to lose directional control.

On open top vehicles the side rails or panels must be at least 910mm (1.21m at the front and back) above the top deck and at least 455mm above the highest part of any seat.

Luggage Racks

These must be constructed so that any article on them, if it becomes dislodged while the vehicle is in motion, is unlikely to fall on the driver or affect his or her control.

Artificial Lighting

Adequate internal illumination must be provided on each deck of a PSV (except in the case of an open-top double-decker) and, on vehicles registered after 1 April 1959, on every step or platform providing an entrance or exit (other than an emergency exit).

On PSVs registered on or after 28 October 1964 there must be a dual lighting circuit so that the failure of either subcircuit does not "black out" either deck.

At least one lamp must be provided as near as is practicable to the top of every staircase leading to the top deck of a double-deck vehicle.

Steps

The lowest entrance step of an unladen PSV must never be more than 435mm (approximately 17 inches) above ground level. However, lower values are required for buses used on local and scheduled services.

Drivers should immediately report:

- a tread case, step, stairway or platform found to be weak or insecure, or excessively worn, or with inadequate anti-slip covering
- a lighting deficiency causing inadequate illumination of step, stairs, platform or interior

- lighting circuits not split, so that a failure of one circuit does not leave part illumination on each deck.

Entrances and Exits

Every vehicle first used after October 1987 must have a *primary* emergency exit of the height of 1.37m leading directly from the saloon of a single-deck bus or the lower deck of a double-deck bus directly to the outside of the vehicle. *Secondary* emergency exits are openings of smaller dimensions. Where only two exits are specified there must be one on either side of the vehicle and there must be an emergency exit on the top deck of double-deckers.

The regulations relating to the minimum number of exits depend on vehicle age and seating capacity.

No. of Seats	Age of Vehicle	Min No. of Exits	
		Primary	Secondary
45 or less	Pre 1981	—	2†
	Post 1981	1	1*
Over 45	Pre 1981	2	1
	Post 1981	1	2*
† one may also serve as a primary exit.			
* one must be of no smaller dimensions than a primary exit.			

In addition, double-deck coaches first used from 1 April 1990 must be fitted with a means of escape in both halves of the vehicle either by the provision of a second staircase or a hammer or other device which can be used to break any side window of the vehicle in case of an emergency. If the latter is to be used it must be displayed in a conspicuous position on the upper deck with an "IN EMERGENCY" sign together with instructions on use nearby.

Note: The main passenger entrance may also qualify as an exit.

Every entrance of a vehicle must be on the nearside but one or more entrances may be placed on the offside (not counting as legally required exits) provided they are fitted with doors controlled by the driver from his or her seat with a controlling device which is clearly separate and distinguishable from any device for opening or closing any entrance door on the nearside. Such doors are often referred to as "Continental Exits" intended for use in countries where vehicles are driven on the right-hand side of the road.

The minimum width of entrances is 530mm.

All emergency exits must be clearly marked both inside and on the outside if they can be opened therefrom, fitted with forward-opening doors and readily accessible to passengers. Emergency exits in single-deck vehicles or on the lower decks of double-deck vehicles must be situated so that passengers can step directly from the gangway to the outside of the vehicle. Manually controlled emergency exit doors must always be unlocked when the vehicle is moving. Emergency exit doors on some moving vehicles can be locked with a speed-related interlock — provided that those doors can be manually opened when the vehicles are stationary. The driver must always check that the gangways are clear.

The means of operation of doors fitted to emergency exits (which must not be power operated) must be clearly indicated and readily accessible to persons of normal height standing outside the vehicle.

Doors

There must be a means of securing the door closed, eg a catch, on every entrance and exit.

If a door on a vehicle is capable of remaining open while the vehicle is in motion, or may be accidentally closed while the vehicle is in motion, there must also be a means of securing it open.

Each door must have two devices (eg handles) for operating it:

- for normal operation, which may be by the vehicle owner or person authorised by him or her, and
- for operating the door from outside the vehicle.

They must be designed to operate with a single movement of the handle and the means of operation must be clearly indicated.

The direction of any manual effort required to operate must be shown (eg "pull to open") and, if the door is power operated, there must be a statement that it may only be used by passengers in an emergency.

If the door operating device is not placed on the door itself:

- it must be placed where it is readily associated with it, and
- its location must be clearly indicated.

All devices must be capable of being operated by a person of normal height (without risk of being struck by the door where the device is not on the door itself) and be so designed that they cannot be accidentally dislodged.

Every door must operate without obstructing access to any entrance or exit from inside or outside the vehicle.

If a door on a vehicle is power operated and projects more than 80mm from the side (excluding any mouldings) when opened it must be interlocked with the transmission so that the vehicle cannot move off with the door open (except when operated in an emergency as above).

The operation of the brakes must be in no way adversely affected by the operation of any power-operated door. If the power-operated system fails, the door must be capable of being opened manually.

On vehicles having power-operated doors, if the interlocking between the door operating mechanism and the transmission, referred to above, is absent, the vertical edges of the doors must be fitted with soft rubber.

All vehicles registered on or after 1 April 1980 with power-operated doors fitted more than 500mm behind the back of the driver's seat must, from 1 April 1993, meet three conditions. The doors must:

- automatically re-open if prevented from closing by an object 60mm high (eg a foot)
- automatically re-open if fingers or a hand are trapped, unless these can be "readily extracted"

- have a "tell tale" light visible to the driver to warn if not fully closed.

Drivers should report immediately if a flap or door has a broken or loose hinge, or is damaged so that it cannot be secured or held open, or has a sharp or protruding edge or defective locking mechanism.

Access to Exits

There must be unobstructed access to at least two exits from every seat in a vehicle (unless the fitness regulations require only a single exit).

This requirement need not be met in the case of:

- any seat beside the driver's seat, accessible by a single entrance other than the driver's door
- a seat on an open top of a double-deck vehicle, having unobstructed access to one exit.

A barrier placed at the foot of the staircase on a double-deck vehicle to prevent passengers riding upstairs (eg in off-peak operation) does not prevent the vehicle complying with this regulation.

No seat may be fitted to any door of a PSV.

Drivers should report immediately if the access to an exit or emergency exit is obstructed (or if the means of breaking any windows designated as emergency exits are missing, inadequate or not clearly marked).

Every gangway on a PSV must be at least 305mm wide at deck level, widening further at "hip" and "shoulder" level. Passages of similar width must be provided between gangways and emergency exits and, on vehicles with seats for more than 12 passengers, gangways must be increased in width to 530mm within 910mm of any entrance or exit.

The minimum prescribed heights of gangways in vehicles adapted to carry more than 12 passengers are as follows.

Single-deck vehicles and lower decks of double-deck vehicles

with 14 or fewer seats	1.6m
with more than 14 seats	1.77m
top deck of double-deck vehicles	1.72m

The minimum height of gangways on vehicles with seats for 12 or fewer passengers is 1.42m reducing to 1.21m at points within 305mm of any entrance or exit.

Drivers should report a dangerously worn or contaminated gangway or entrance mat.

Seating

The supports of all seats must be securely fixed in position.

Each seat must have a closed back rest designed to prevent passengers' pockets being picked from behind.

The positioning of seats on PSVs is governed by the minimum dimensions shown.

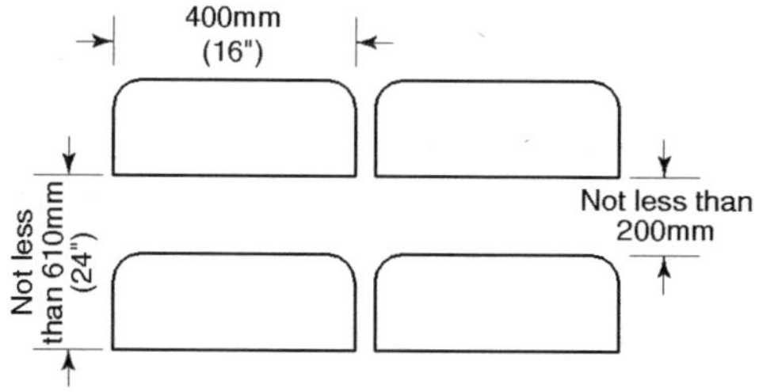

There must be protection, in the form of a guard rail or screen, for seated passengers, where there is any likelihood of their being thrown against an entrance or exit.

The front of any seat must not be any closer than 225mm to any well or step.

Drivers should report:

- distorted or fractured seat frames

- insecure seating
- insecure fittings or arm rests having sharp projections
- dirty or damaged seat coverings
- dirty or defective seat belts.

Courier seats

Crew seats (as the regulations describe these folding seats) may now be fitted at the front of PSVs.

The requirements for the construction and use of courier/crew seats are that they must be provided with arm rests and a suitable place for the occupant to rest his or her feet. There must be at least 300mm clear space in front of the leading edge of the crew seat and, whether in or out of use, the crew seat must not impede the driver's field of vision. When in use it is permissible for the crew seat to protrude into the gangway but those parts which do protrude must automatically retract when the seat is not in use.

The words "for crew use only" must be marked on or near each crew seat in letters at least 10mm tall.

Driver's Accommodation

The driver must have a means of preventing light from the vehicle interior disturbing him or her, and, if the vehicle has more than 12 seats, the driver's seat must be adjustable both vertically and horizontally.

Where access to this seat is from the offside, the means of entry must be at least 455mm wide and provided with a grab handle and step if the entrance is more than 690mm above the ground. If the cab is enclosed there must be an emergency escape window at least 530mm × 455mm other than on the offside.

On all vehicles with more than 12 passenger seats where access to the driver's seat is by means of a passage, the passage must be at least 300mm wide.

Ventilation

This must be adequate for driver and passengers without the need to open a window to demist the windscreen. Drivers should report missing, inoperative or blocked demisting and ventilating equipment.

Windscreens

These must be capable of being opened to give the driver a clear view ahead unless there is an adequate demisting and defrosting device. In practice the demisting requirement is normally met.

Signals

A means of signalling the driver to stop must be provided on passenger vehicles with 12 or more seats. Drivers should report any broken or missing system of passenger communication.

EQUIPMENT OF PSVs

Fire Extinguishers and First Aid

Every PSV must carry a fire extinguisher to British Standard EN3 containing water or AFFF (foam). Every vehicle on non-local services must carry a first aid box suitable for storing the items referred to.

These must be:

- readily available for use
- clearly marked as a first aid box, or, if a fire extinguisher, with the appropriate BSI specification number
- maintained in good order.

The items to be carried in the first aid box, which must be of good and reliable quality and suitable design, are:

- 10 antiseptic wipes, foil packed
- one conforming disposable bandage (not less than 7.5cm wide)

- two triangular bandages
- one packet of 24 assorted adhesive dressings
- three large sterile unmedicated ambulance dressings (not less than 15cm × 20cm)
- two sterile eye pads, with attachments
- 12 assorted safety pins
- one pair of rustless blunt-ended scissors.

A first aid box which is inaccessible, obviously in poor condition, illegibly marked or missing, and a fire extinguisher which is inaccessible, obviously discharged or missing, should be immediately reported by the driver.

USE OF PSVs

Obstruction of Entrances, Exits and Gangways

No unnecessary obstruction to the above must be caused or permitted while passengers are being carried.

Obstruction of Driver

No person shall cause or permit any unnecessary obstruction to the driver.

Body Maintenance

Vehicles must not be used to carry passengers unless the windows, fittings and seats are in a clean and good condition.

Lamps

If carrying passengers during the hours of darkness, vehicles must have sufficient lights operating to illuminate the access to all seats and exits and any emergency exit markings. This may be extinguished on the upper deck of a double-deck vehicle if a barrier is secured at the foot of all stairways.

Power-operated Doors

Except in an emergency, power-operated doors may only be operated by the driver or by some other person authorised by the operator, and then not if the vehicle is in motion.

Carriage of Conductors

No vehicle with more than 20 seats may be used on a local service without a conductor unless:

- it is a single-deck vehicle with seats for fewer than 32 passengers and the emergency exit is at the front of the vehicle, visible to the driver and the entrance is also visible so that the driver is aware of any passenger trapped in the door, or
- it has been certified for driver-only operation under the code of practice for One Person Operation (OPO).

Carriage of Flammable or Dangerous Substances

In addition to any requirements under petroleum or similar regulations, flammable or dangerous substances may only be carried if in containers designed and constructed to minimise the risk of damage to the vehicle or injury to passengers in the event of an accident. Such containers might be used to carry a personal oxygen supply for asthmatic passengers.

Markings

The name and address of the authority, company or individual to whom the PSV "O" licence was issued and their principal place of business must be marked on the vehicle's nearside in a conspicuous position, in clearly legible characters at least 25mm tall, in colours contrasting with their background. Similarly the seating and standing capacity must be marked on the inside.

All emergency exits should be marked both inside and outside the vehicle.

Missing or illegible statutory markings should be reported by the driver.

School Bus Signs

Buses and/or coaches with nine or more passenger seats being used to transport children under the age of 16 to or from school at the start and finish of the school day must display a school bus sign. Drivers may also use hazard warning lights when pupils are embarking or disembarking from the vehicle.

The regulations do not apply where the children are travelling on a vehicle being used to provide a registered service (so long as this is not an excursion or tour) or services which cover local registered services where 50% or more of the seats are available to the general public, or London local services (see *Chapter 2*).

The school bus sign does not have to be removed when children are not being carried.

6 DRIVERS' HOURS, WORKING TIME AND TACHOGRAPH LEGISLATION

Drivers of passenger carrying vehicles (PCV) are legally restricted on the number of hours they can drive and/or work, which is dependent upon the type of work they undertake. At the same time the legislation controls the minimum amount of break or rest the driver must take before resuming work or driving.

The purpose of the legislation is threefold, to:

- harmonise conditions of competition
- improve working conditions for the driver
- improve road safety.

The nature of work being undertaken will dictate which piece(s) of legislation the driver will be required to comply with on a daily and/or weekly basis. These are:

- EU Drivers' Hours Regulation (561/2006) (as amended)
- EU Tachograph Legislation (3821/85 as amended)
- EU Working Time (Road Transport) Directive (2002/15/EC)
- GB Domestic Drivers' Hours Regulations (the 1968 Transport Act relaxed by Drivers' Hours (Passenger & Goods Vehicles) (Modifications) Order 1971).

WHICH REGULATIONS SHOULD BE ADHERED TO?

The EU Drivers' Hours Regulation applies to the carriage of passengers by vehicles that are constructed to carry more than nine persons, including the driver. Therefore, unless the particular journey type is exempt from the EU rules, the driver must comply with them. In addition, the driver will be required to comply with the Working Time Directive.

Exemptions

There are, however, a number of types of operations that will be exempt from the regulations. Some of these exemptions are fixed, while others are dependent upon the Member State. Within Great Britain the Government makes the possible derogation reality.

Therefore the regulations relating to the EU Drivers' Hours legislation do not apply to carriage by road by the following.

1. Vehicles used for the carriage of passengers on regular services where the route covered by the service in question does not exceed 50km. (This, therefore, relates to specific scheduled routes and will generally apply to the local bus services seen within most towns and cities. However, where the passenger service is in the form of a block booking, for example from a tour operator which provides a journey from an airport or another location to a hotel where the precise route to be taken was not specified and therefore predetermined, has been held by a court not to constitute a regular service within the meaning of the regulation as stated in the case of *E Clarke & Son (Coaches) Ltd, The Times,* 1 May 1998, EQ. These services therefore would by interpretation not be exempt).
2. Vehicles with a maximum authorised speed not exceeding 40km per hour.
3. Vehicles owned or hired without a driver by the armed services, civil defence services, fire services, and forces responsible for maintaining public order when the carriage is undertaken as a consequence of the tasks assigned to these services and is under their control.
4. Vehicles, including vehicles used in the non-commercial transport of humanitarian aid, used in emergencies or rescue operations.
5. Specialised vehicles used for medical purposes.

6. Specialised breakdown vehicles operating within a 100km radius of their base.
7. Vehicles undergoing road tests for technical development, repair or maintenance purposes, and new or rebuilt vehicles which have not yet been put into service.
8. Vehicles or combinations of vehicles with a maximum permissible mass not exceeding 7.5 tonnes used for the non-commercial carriage of goods.
9. Commercial vehicles that have a historic status according to the legislation of the Member State in which they are being driven and that are used for the non-commercial carriage of passengers or goods. *For the purpose of Article 3(i) of the Community Drivers' Hours Regulation a vehicle has a historic status if it is a vehicle which is by virtue of its construction and equipment suitable for carrying passengers or goods and which was manufactured more than 25 years before the date on which it is being driven, but it is essential that its use is of a non-commercial nature.*

MEMBER STATE EXEMPTION

The EU Drivers' Hours legislation from 11 April 2007 allows Member States to adopt further categories of vehicles as being exempt from the regulation providing the purpose of the legislation is not jeopardised.

It would appear that, as a consequence, the following categories of PCV vehicles will also be exempt from the regulation.

1. Vehicles owned or hired, without a driver, by public authorities to undertake carriage by road that do not compete with private transport undertakings; *this will tend to cover only those vehicles used by*:
   (a) health authorities to carry staff, patients or equipment
   (b) local authorities to provide for the elderly or handicapped
   (c) coastguards and lighthouse services

(d) harbours and airports providing that the vehicle remains within the port or airport on roads which are not open to the public.

2. Vehicles or combinations of vehicles with a maximum permissible mass not exceeding 7.5 tonnes used:
   (a) for driving instruction and examination with a view to obtaining a driving licence or a certificate of professional competence, provided that they are not being used for the commercial carriage of goods or passengers
   (b) exclusively for the non-commercial carriage of passengers with between 10 and 17 seats.

The main exemption for a PCV where the EU Drivers' Hours Regulation does not apply, but GB Domestic Drivers' Hours legislation will apply is when vehicles are used for the carriage of passengers on regular services where the route covered by the service in question does not exceed 50 kilometres.

This therefore relates to specific scheduled routes and will generally apply to the local bus services seen within most towns and cities. However, these regular services may be for specific to a group of individuals, ie a school service or transportation for a specific group of workers to and from work on a daily basis.

The main derogation is that vehicles with between 10 and 17 seats used exclusively for the non-commercial carriage of passengers will also be exempt.

Please note that the movement of empty vehicles from one location to another (placement journey) may or may not come under the EU Drivers' Hours Regulation. This is generally dependent upon the activity the vehicle was undertaking before and/or after the "placement journey".

For example:

If a vehicle is to be moved from a depot to another location at which another driver takes over on a journey which would come under the EU Drivers' Hours Regulation. Where that vehicle has to travel on the "placement journey", even for a short period on a road, even where that journey is undertaken by a person who in the normal course of his working day is undertaking yard duties or another activity other than driving, the vehicle is not exempt and a tachograph must be used for that person making the "placement journey" on each day they undertake this activity. This tachograph record must show not only the driver's recordings whilst in the vehicle, but also, a manual record for the whole of the working day. Furthermore, the driver will also have to comply with the Daily Rest Regulations on that day and before that shift, and the Weekly Rest Regulations for that week.

Alternatively, if the driver is required to drive the vehicle to a location to commence a journey along a scheduled route of less than 50km, ie where the driver would then work under GB Domestic Drivers' Hours regulations, then the "placement journey" would also come under domestic regulations.

THE TACHOGRAPH

Since the introduction of tachographs in Great Britain on 1 January 1982, the nature and characteristic of tachographs has evolved, particularly in the last 10–15 years and at the moment there are three broadly different models.

1. *The hinged tachograph* — this is in the position of the traditional speedometer and opens using a key for a traditional analogue wax-coated disc which is inserted.
2. *The CD-style tachograph* — which opens with a drawer into which a traditional analogue wax-coated disc is inserted.
3. *The digital tachograph* — in which is inserted the driver's digital card, which stores the relevant data and is downloaded for the purpose of record keeping, which was required to be fitted to all new vehicles registered on or after 1 May 2006.

Each of these models records the required data using different methods.

The earlier tachograph heads, known as analogue tachographs (1 and 2), incorporate three, or in the newer models, two styli to record, against time, on the circular disc, the traditional tachograph chart, the speed of the vehicle, the distance travelled and the driver's selected activity. Each chart covers a period of 24 hours.

The digital tachograph (3) is slightly different, recording various aspects including the driver's activity against time, but speed is only recorded for the last 24 hours of movement of the vehicle and this, instead of being recorded on the driver's digital card is stored on the Vehicle Unit (VU). The company can recover this speed data, along with other information from the Vehicle Unit.

Important Where a driver is required to use a tachograph then he or she must ensure that the chart or data record shows a record for a complete "daily working period".

A Daily Working Period comprises the driving time, other work, periods of availability and periods of break or rest taken as part of the working day.

The record, whether this is analogue or digital, must show a complete record of these activities from the end of the previous daily or weekly rest period to the start of the next daily or weekly rest period.

So, there may be occasions where the working day is longer than the recordings made automatically on the chart or driver's digital card. As an example, a driver may attend work and undertake yard duties before having access to his or her own vehicle. Where this occurs, then when accessing the vehicle the driver must make a manual record on the grid on the reverse of the analogue chart or, by using the series of buttons and put a manual record on the driver's digital card.

The day does not necessarily start or end when the driver inserts and removes the chart/driver card. In many cases prosecutions are based on the difference between a driver's claimed working times as shown on a time-sheet or clocking-on machine which differs from the recordings on the tachograph record. In these circumstances penalties may be a maximum of £5000 and will result in the driver being called to a driver conduct hearing with the Traffic Commissioner to determine whether the driver is a "fit and proper" person to hold a vocational licence.

Details of the likely action to be taken by the Traffic Commissioner can be found on the VOSA website at *www.gov.uk/vosa*.

Placement Journeys

Placement journeys may not simply involve transferring a vehicle from the depot to the start point of the service route or private hire; they may also be to transport the driver to a position from the driver's usual operating base or home to take over a vehicle from a location other than where he or she is normally based.

1. If the driver has to travel, even in what would appear to be his or her own time, for example, as a feeder driver to meet a coach en route, then that time spent travelling is part of the daily working period. For example, if the vehicle is to be collected from a motorway service area or ferry terminal and the driver has an hour journey to get there then that one hour travelling time is to be recorded. This would be considered as Other Work activity if the driver is driving a car, van or any non-tachograph vehicle to that point, or as a period of availability, if he or she was travelling as a passenger. This time must be recorded manually on the appropriate tachograph record, whether the driver is paid or not, as he or she is not freely able to dispose of time to fulfil the company's requirements.
2. Similarly, if at the end of the day the driver is required to leave the vehicle at a location other than the vehicle's operating centre or driver's base then the journey back to the depot, or home must be recorded manually on the tachograph record, as the working day does not end until the driver returns to that point.

Analogue Tachographs

Chart centre-field — drivers' responsibilities — before driving
The driver must also complete the centre-field of the tachograph chart, both before and at the end of the journey. Before commencing the journey the driver must enter:

- name (surname and first name)
- the start point — this must be a recognised map location name. Where a driver has stopped in a major city, eg London, this is too general and should be an area, eg Battersea or postcode, eg London NE17. Alternatively, it is not necessary to be too precise, eg a street name
- opening odometer reading
- vehicle registration number
- date of chart insertion.

Note: Tachograph charts must be used for all instances where drivers work mixed duties, ie duties involving domestic and EU driving and cover the full extent of the working day.

Recording Daily Rest and any activity — up to the point at which the driver takes over the vehicle. This can be done by drawing a line round from 0000 hours to the time work commenced on the grid on the back of the chart, followed, if applicable, by any activity undertaken until the chart is inserted.

It is recommended that drivers also enter times when the work began with the letters indicated below to indicate whether they have ended a weekly or daily rest.

EDR end daily rest

EWR end weekly rest

The images for chart completion for the front and back of the chart are shown on pages 122 and 123.

Make sure the clock is set correctly
Clocks on analogue tachographs must be set to the time in the country of registration for that vehicle. If the clock is set incorrectly, and this is identified on entering the vehicle, then the clock should be adjusted accordingly at that time.

However, if it is noticed part way through a shift that the clock is set incorrectly then do not adjust the clock at that time. This will create either a gap in the recordings or an overlap of the traces. Make a note and then at the end of the use of that chart make a note on the back detailing the time error and only then adjust the clock accordingly.

Insert the tachograph chart into tachograph

It is the driver's responsibility to ensure that the chart is inserted correctly and that includes being the correct way up and not damaged before or on insertion (otherwise, some or all recordings will not be made or will be made on the wrong section of the chart and this is an offence).

When stationary, select the mode symbol appropriate to the activity:

- Other Work
- Periods of Availability
- Break.

Details of the use of modes is given on p.126 under *Work Modes*.

If the tachograph develops a fault during shift

- Remove chart as soon as possible.
- Record remainder of shift activities manually on the reverse side of the chart.
- Make a note of the defect and report it to the operator as soon as possible.

If the chart becomes damaged

- Replace with a new chart and keep together (but not stapled) to make a complete record at the end of the shift — by law drivers must return all dirty and damaged charts to the operator. If due to damage or fault any of the record is missing then the driver must make a manual record of the unrecorded period.

At the end of the shift

The driver should:

- check that the chart is fully completed for the shift and on the chart complete:
  - the location at which the work ends for the driver
  - the date on which the work ends, even if it is the same date as work commenced
  - the closing odometer reading.

The total distance covered in the working period is optional.

Having removed the chart, drivers should check that:

- breaks have been recorded and that the correct mode has been selected during stationary periods
- all gaps in the recordings are covered with manual entries on the back of the chart
- times are entered on the grid on the back of the chart, when the work ended, with the letters indicated below to indicate whether they have commenced a weekly or daily rest and manually any activity from the chart removal to the time of the end of the shift.

SDR start daily rest

SWR start weekly rest

When changing vehicles

- Take the chart out of the tachograph and take it to the next vehicle, then:
  - on removing the chart from the first vehicle enter the closing odometer reading for the first vehicle in the space provided
  - at that time, the driver should *not* complete the finish place or finish date, these belong to the whole chart and not just the first vehicle and should be completed at the end of the shift.
- Enter the details of the vehicle change on the chart in the spaces provided, ie:
  - the time the driver takes over the new vehicle
  - the new vehicle registration
  - the odometer readings when taking over and leaving the vehicle.
- Manually record activities between vehicles.

- Insert the chart into the tachograph of the new vehicle and set the mode switch to record the correct activity when stationary.

If the chart has been removed because someone else may move the vehicle, ie it has been taken in for maintenance/calibration, then treat this as a change of vehicle.

Chart retention

- Drivers *must* keep with them, as a minimum, their analogue charts completed for the current day and the preceding 28 calendar days.
- The legal maximum limit is 42 days and therefore within 42 days from use all charts must be returned to the operator.

Lost charts

- If charts are lost or stolen then drivers must produce a manual record of the days missing.
- These manual records must be as accurate as possible and made in conjunction with further documentation to prove their accuracy.
- If stolen then a police reference number should be entered on the chart.

To enable easier understanding an example of a typical chart completion is given on pages 122 and 123.

Digital Tachographs

Digital tachographs are used together with a driver's digital card.

Drivers' card

This card holds a minimum of 28 days of data recording the driver's various activities over that period, along with distance and any recent events and faults. Please note that this is a minimum of 28 days and, in reality, the driver card stores several months' data. Even when downloaded the data is copied and not wiped and the data for all that period will therefore be retained on the driver's card.

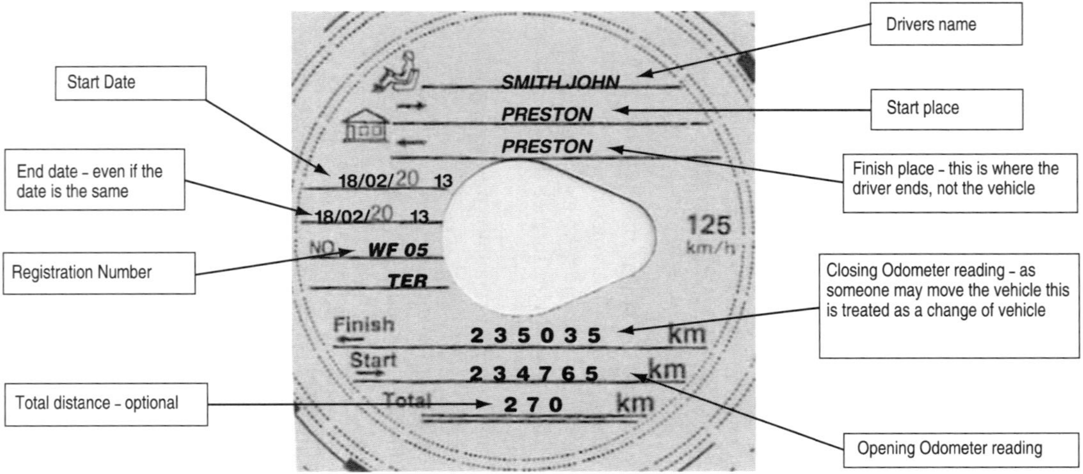
Drivers name
Start place
Finish place - this is where the driver ends, not the vehicle
Closing Odometer reading - as someone may move the vehicle this is treated as a change of vehicle
Opening Odometer reading
Start Date
End date - even if the date is the same
Registration Number
Total distance - optional
SMITH JOHN
PRESTON
PRESTON
18/02/20 13
18/02/20 13
NO WF 05
TER
125
km/h
Finish
2 3 5 0 3 5 km
Start
2 3 4 7 6 5 km
Total
2 7 0 km

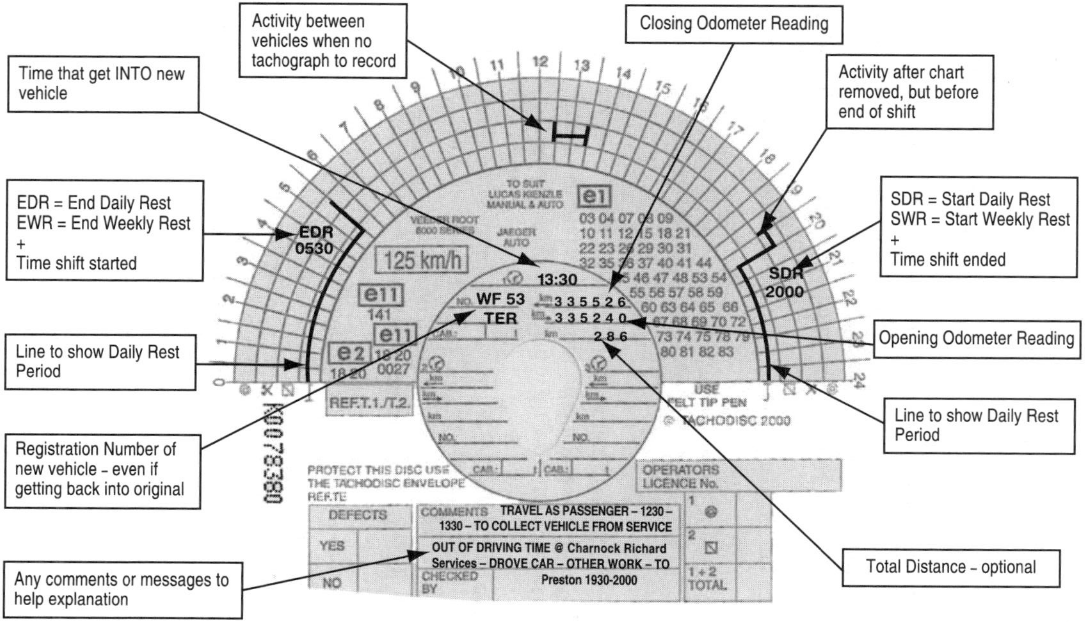

Time that get INTO new vehicle
Activity between vehicles when no tachograph to record
Closing Odometer Reading
Activity after chart removed, but before end of shift
EDR = End Daily Rest
EWR = End Weekly Rest
+
Time shift started
SDR = Start Daily Rest
SWR = Start Weekly Rest
+
Time shift ended
EDR 0530
SDR 2000
13:30
WF 53 TER
3 3 5 5 2 6
3 3 5 2 4 0
2 8 6
125 km/h
Line to show Daily Rest Period
Opening Odometer Reading
Line to show Daily Rest Period
Registration Number of new vehicle - even if getting back into original
TRAVEL AS PASSENGER – 1230 – 1330 – TO COLLECT VEHICLE FROM SERVICE
OUT OF DRIVING TIME @ Charnock Richard Services – DROVE CAR – OTHER WORK – TO Preston 1930-2000
Any comments or messages to help explanation
Total Distance - optional

The card is personal to the driver concerned and is valid for five years. It should be noted that it is simpler to process a driver card application if a photo-card driving licence is held.

If the driver has been issued with a Driver's Digital Tachograph Card, he or she must carry this at all times when on duty, even if driving an analogue tachograph vehicle.

The maximum period between downloads of data is 28 days, although it is recommended that downloads are undertaken on a more regular basis.

If a driver card malfunctions, is lost, stolen or damaged a replacement card must be applied for within seven calendar days. Only under exceptional circumstances may a driver drive for longer than 15 days without a digital card. This can only occur where the driver can prove it was necessary for the vehicle to return to its premises and during that time he or she can prove the impossibility of producing or using the card during this period.

If a driver has never been issued with a digital card he or she cannot drive a digital vehicle undertaking work under the EU Drivers' Hours Regulation until his or her first digital card has been received.

Manual entries and activities

When a driver inserts the digital card following a period of rest or being away from the vehicle, the vehicle unit will prompt to enter details of missing periods of working time since the card was last removed.

Please note: this is the one and only opportunity to write manual entries to the driver's digital card for that missing period — therefore it is advised that clear note of any manual entries that the driver wishes to make is made in order to refer to these whilst making the entries.

As with analogue records the driver must make a complete record of his or her daily working period, ie the period between two daily rest periods or between a daily and weekly rest period. Any missing activity during a shift is an incomplete record and an offence.

UTC Time (Universal Time Co-ordinated)

Digital tachographs are set to record in UTC time.

UK Winter time (Greenwich Mean Time) = UTC time.

UTC time is 1 hour behind during UK summer time (BST), ie between the last Sunday in March to last Sunday in October.

The driver must make allowances for this, where applicable (some later models allow entries in local time rather than UTC), in all driver records and manual inputs.

Data stored and shown on printouts are also in UTC time and this must be remembered and accounted for when mixing the use with analogue tachographs or manual records.

Digital tachograph malfunction, lost or stolen cards

If the driver's digital card is lost, stolen or defective then the driver must take a printout from the Vehicle Unit at the start and end of each shift. This can be done by entering the menu on the digital tachograph and scrolling to "printout vehicle" and then printing the "24h" printout for the current day.

Where appropriate the driver should make the correct manual records on the back of the printout and must also continue to use the Work Mode correctly as this data is still stored on the Vehicle Unit.

Signing print-outs

Any print-out being used for the recording of data required by law must show on the reverse of the print-out, in the spaces provided, the driver's name, his or her digital card number, the date, the driver's signature and also record the DVLA reference number if provided.

Retention of print-outs

All print-outs being used to show data required to be recorded by the driver must be retained by the driver in the same way as the tachograph charts, ie for the current day and the preceding 28 calendar days and up to a maximum 42 days before being returned to the operator.

Validity of driver card

A driver's digital card is only valid until the expiry date shown. A driver's application for a replacement card must arrive at the DVLA at least 15 days before the old card is due to expire. Failure to do so will mean that if the replacement card has not arrived by the time the current card expires a driver cannot drive a digital tachograph vehicle under EU regulations until such time as the replacement card has arrived.

Having received the replacement driver's digital card the driver should continue to use his or her original card up to the date at which it is due to expire. Then on commencing using the replacement card from its start date the driver must still carry the previous card for a further 28 days as this will hold the data for the required retention period.

WORK MODES

Important points — the work modes are now defined but please remember:

- a tachograph is only semi-automatic — when stationary it cannot tell whether the driver is having a cup of tea or loading or unloading passengers or baggage or waiting in a queue — the driver has to tell it
- the driver must use the work mode and check this every time he or she is stationary and at the end of the day to make sure the recordings are accurate — this is a legal requirement — the recordings must be a true record of the working day.

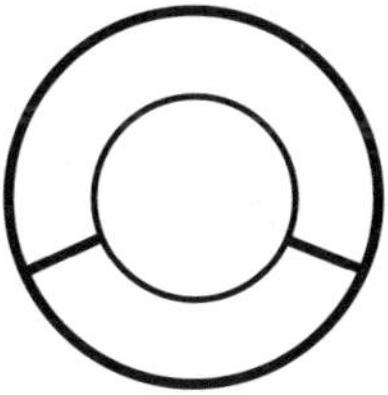

Driving = the steering wheel — is for driving time and counts towards the working time for the purpose of Working Time Directive for mobile workers — this will be automatically activated when the vehicle moves to record all driving activity, but if the tachograph is defective then use this mode to show driving in a PCV under the EU regulations.

Other work = crossed hammers — counts towards the working time for the Working Time Directive — What counts as Other Work:

- loading/unloading of passengers or luggage
- training for the purpose of their work
- cleaning and technical maintenance
- work intended for the safety of the vehicle or its load — this means vehicle checks must be recorded using crossed hammers
- work to fulfil the legal or regulatory obligations directly linked to a specific operation under way including monitoring of loading/unloading, administrative formalities with police/customs, etc
- waiting time where the duration of the wait is not known
- driving a car on a placement journey is Other Work, not Periods of Availability (PoA) — this must be recorded on the grid on the reverse of the chart or by manual entry on the next digital driver card insertion.

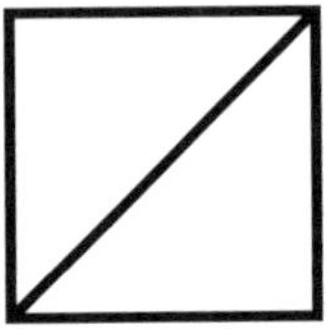

POA = Square with line through — generally for waiting time – when the driver knows the length of the delay or travelling as a passenger.

Break and daily rest periods = Bed Symbol — a break is "any period during which a driver may not carry out any driving or any other work and which is used exclusively for recuperation".

EU DRIVING PERIODS AND DRIVING BREAKS

Daily and Weekly Driving

- The daily driving period should not exceed nine hours per day.
- However, on two occasions in a fixed week (a fixed week being defined as being from 0000 hours on a Monday until 2400 hours the following Sunday) the driver may extend this 9-hour daily driving limit to no more than 10 hours driving per day.
- The weekly driving time shall not exceed 56 hours and shall not result in the maximum weekly working time laid down in the Working Time Directive (60 hours working time) being exceeded.

A week, as stated, is from 0000 on a Monday to 2400 hours the following Sunday. Therefore in a week a driver, for example, may drive:

Day		Driving Time
Monday	—	9 hours
Tuesday	—	9 hours
Wednesday	—	10 hours
Thursday	—	10 hours
Friday	—	9 hours
Saturday	—	9 hours

Weekly Driving Time = 56 hours in a week

However, it is important that a driver is aware that the weekly driving time is not calculated within the driver's working week, but within the legal fixed week, which as stated above is from 0000 hours on a Monday until 2400 hours the following Sunday and therefore the example below is illegal.

Day	Driving Time	Weekly Total
Monday	9 hours	9
Tuesday	9 hours	18
Wednesday	10 hours	28
Thursday	10 hours	38
Friday	9 hours	47
Saturday	9 hours	56
Weekly Rest Period — 24 hours		
Sunday	3 hours	59

Weekly Drive Time = 59 hours **illegal**

This is illegal, as although the driver is now in another working week the law applies to the legal fixed week and the 56-hour weekly limit has been exceeded.

Two-weekly Driving Limit

To prevent drivers driving 56 hours each week under EU Drivers' Hours Regulation there is a driving limit in any two consecutive weeks.

This states that in any two consecutive weeks (0000 hours on a Monday until 2400 hours two Sunday's later) a driver may not drive in excess of 90 hours.

Therefore in three weeks there are two fortnightly driving periods to be calculated, for example:

Week 1 + Week 2 is one period and Week 2 + Week 3 is the next period.

In the table below there is a two-weekly driving hours' offence:

Day	**Week 1**	**Week 2**	**Week 3**
Monday	8	9	10
Tuesday	9	10	8
Wednesday	9	10	8
Thursday	10	9	9
Friday	7	Rest	9
Saturday	7	Rest	Rest
Sunday	Rest	8	Rest
Weekly Total	**50**	**46**	**44**

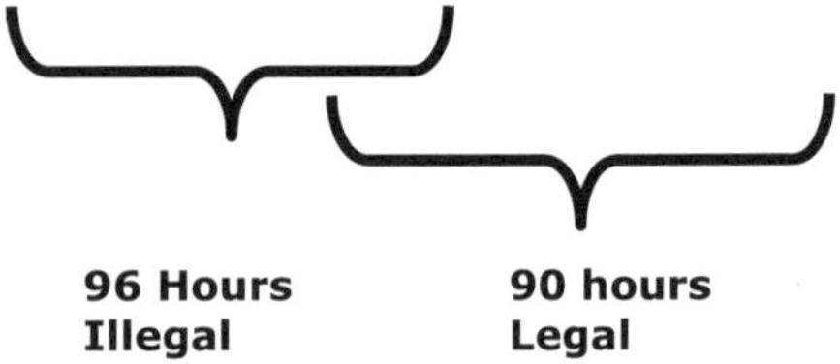

In the period between 0000 hours on the Monday of Week 1 to 2400 hours of the Sunday at the end of week 2 the driver has driven 96 hours in this two week period and therefore this is illegal. Therefore, the driver should have stopped after two hours driving on the Sunday of week 2 to remain legal. This also shows that although the driver has taken a weekly rest period this does not clear the two-weekly driving limit.

Note: In the other two-week period, namely Week 2 and Week 3 (where 90 hours driving was undertaken) the fortnightly driving limit has not been exceeded.

If a driver is driving exclusively in a digital tachograph vehicle throughout a two-week period, under EU regulations, then they can use the data on their digital card to display the two-weekly driving total.

Continuous Driving

After a driving period of 4½ hours the driver will take an uninterrupted break of not less than 45 minutes, unless he or she begins a rest period.

Note: Unlike the remainder of Europe, within Great Britain, the enforcement body, VOSA, does not currently consider Periods of Availability (PoA) as being a driving break. This is particularly important for drivers using a digital vehicle as the digital tachograph will consider a PoA as being a driving break and therefore should the driver take 45 minutes PoA this will wipe the accumulated driving time since the last valid driving break back to zero, but it will not be interpreted in this manner by VOSA. In those circumstances the driver must calculate the 4½-hour driving period themselves and not rely upon the tachograph for its calculation.

If a driver reaches exactly 4½ hours driving he or she must not do any other activity until the required break is fully completed.

Therefore, if a driver undertook the scenario below he or she would be committing a contravention.

Other Work	— 1 hour
Driving	— 4½ hours
Other Work	— **½ hour**
Break	— 45 minutes

Having completed 4½ hours driving the break of 45 minutes should have been taken immediately.

A break is when the driver can use the time "exclusively for recuperation", ie eat, drink, read a paper. Breaks do not constitute, for example, time spent in a traffic queue and moving up at regular intervals, loading, unloading or where the driver must remain with the vehicle to undertake another activity.

Accumulated Driving with Breaks

This is similar to the continuous driving above in that the driver may accumulate up to 4½ hours driving time rather than driving continuously for that period before taking a break.

Where this occurs the 45 minutes break may be replaced by a first break of at least 15 minutes followed by a break of at least 30 minutes each distributed over the period in such a way as to comply with the provisions of the continuous driving, ie 45 minutes break to a maximum driving period of 4½ hours.

Note: On some older digital tachographs, the pre-2007 regulations are set in the software and therefore drivers may be advised they were legal, but this is not the case; similarly if the digital tachographs allow a PoA as a break and therefore again these would advise the driver he or she was legal when VOSA would identify a breach of the regulations.

As examples:

If the first break was 29 minutes the second break must still be at least 30 minutes
If the first break was 22 minutes the second break must still be at least 30 minutes
If the first break was 20 minutes the second break must still be at least 30 minutes
If the first break was 44 minutes the second break must still be at least 30 minutes

The current interpretation is that when a driver completes a 45-minute break, either as a single break of 45 minutes or as two breaks, the first of at least 15 minutes and the second of at least 30 minutes, during or at the end of the 4½-hour period, the calculation of the driving time should begin afresh, without taking account of the driving time and breaks previously completed.

As a result this means that if a break of 45 minutes or more is taken, whether in one block or totalling at least 45 minutes in two periods, the first of which is of at least 15 minutes, the second of which must be at least 30 minutes, a new 4½-hour driving period commences, regardless of the previous driving time before these breaks.

Below are a number of examples of driving and breaks.

These show some examples that are legal and others that are illegal.

Example 1

Drive	—	2½ hours
Break	—	30 minutes
Drive	—	2 hours
Break	—	**15 minutes**
Drive	—	1 hour

This is illegal as the driver has taken a 30-minute break, which complies with the requirement for the first break to be at least 15 minutes, but the second break must be of at least 30 minutes and, in this example, the second break is only 15 minutes and therefore this would result in the driver having driven 5½ hours, but only 30 minutes break has been taken as the second break is only 15 minutes.

Example 2

Drive	—	2 hours
Break	—	45 minutes
Drive	—	2½ hours
Break	—	30 minutes
Drive	—	2 hours
Break	—	**15 minutes**
Drive	—	1 hour

After the 45-minute break the slate is wiped clean and a new 4½-hour driving period commences.

However, after that there follows a period where some 5½ hours driving has occurred, but only 30 minutes of qualifying breaks are taken as the second break, in bold, is only 15 minutes and the second break should be at least 30 minutes. Therefore, this is illegal.

Example 3

Drive	—	2 hours
Break	—	**45 minutes — point A**
Drive	—	2½ hours
Break	—	15 minutes
Drive	—	2 hours
Break	—	**30 minutes — point B**
Drive	—	1 hour

After the 45-minute break, at **Point A**, the slate is wiped clean and a new 4½-hour driving period commences. This time there is a 15-minute break which is then followed by a second break which is of 30 minutes, at **Point B**, after the 4½ hours driving period made up of the 2½ hours and 2 hours driving, thereby meeting the criteria of the law and this example is therefore legal.

Note: Remember the 4½ hours driving is a maximum limit and the 45-minute break is a minimum.

Daily Rest

Regular daily rest

A driver must have at least 11 consecutive hours daily rest in the 24 hours from when work begins and this is known as a "regular daily rest period".

The daily rest period may be reduced to a minimum of nine consecutive hours rest in 24 hours from when work begins on no more than three occasions between two weekly rest periods — the working week.

This therefore means that the daily rest period can be between 9–11 consecutive hours in the 24 hours from when work begins on no more than three occasions between two weekly rest periods.

Reductions in daily rest periods do not need to be compensated.

A daily rest may only be taken in a vehicle if it has suitable sleeping arrangements and is stationary. A daily rest cannot be taken on a moving vehicle, other than a ferry or train and even then the driver must have access to suitable sleeping arrangements.

If the driver is "at rest" in the vehicle, but the vehicle is being driven by a crew member, or any other person, then this is not a daily rest, nor is taking the vehicle to get some food; the vehicle MUST be stationary throughout the daily rest period.

As mentioned above the daily rest must be calculated within the 24 hours period from when work commences. This is an area in which many drivers regularly contravene through ignorance of the law, but ignorance is *no defence.*

If the spreadover is longer than 13 hours the maximum rest that can be taken in the 24 hours from when work begins has to be less than 11 hours and therefore this is a reduction even if the driver has then taken a rest period of 11 hours between shifts.

For example, if a driver starts work on a Monday at 0600 hours and undertakes a 14 hours working day until 2000 hours that evening and the driver then begins on the Tuesday at 0700 hours; many drivers will calculate the daily rest between 2000–0700 and consider this as an 11-hour daily rest period.

However, the daily rest can only ever be calculated in the 24 hours from when work began and therefore as the working day began at 0600 hours on the Monday the calculation stops at 0600 hours on the Tuesday and therefore there are 10 hours consecutive rest between 2000 hours and 0600 hours and this is a reduction.

Furthermore, to get 9 hours consecutive rest in the 24 hours from when work began, the minimum permitted rest, if the daily spreadover is greater than 15 hours then the driver cannot get 9 hours consecutive rest in the 24 hours from when work began. For example if the driver begins work at 0700 hours on the Tuesday then by 0700 hours on the Wednesday the daily rest calculation stops. Therefore, if the driver works until 2230 hours on the Tuesday, even if he doesn't work at all on the Wednesday, from 2230 hours on Tuesday, until 0700 hours on Wednesday is only 8½ hours and this is therefore below the minimum permitted in the 24 hours from when work began even though the driver did not work at all the next day.

Where drivers do not apply the split daily rest regulation (which is described below) then the driver's daily working period (spreadover) is 13 hours, but this may be increased on a *maximum* of three occasions between two weekly rest periods to a maximum spreadover of 15 hours, *but this will depend on the start time each day*.

The table below shows how a driver, by taking a reduced daily rest after *a short working day on two occasions in a week*, can then only work one day where the spreadover exceeds 13 hours. When he or she works a second day over 13 hours on the Friday, because the driver has already used up the three reductions, an offence is committed. Therefore, a driver must calculate the daily rest in two ways; what is the longest rest taken in the 24 hours from when work begins, and the difference from the end of one shift to the start of the next, whichever is the shorter is the driver's daily rest period.

Split daily rest periods

This counts as a "regular daily rest period" and is therefore not a reduction even though the longest rest period in 24 hours may be as low as 9 hours.

For a split daily rest the driver must comply with certain basic rules:

- the rest may be split into no more than *two periods*
- the first period must be of *at least 3 hours*
- the last period of rest must be of *at least 9 hours*
- the total rest period *in 24 hours must be of at least 12 hours*
- there are no reductions permitted when the rest is being taken in this format.

Daily Rest Periods

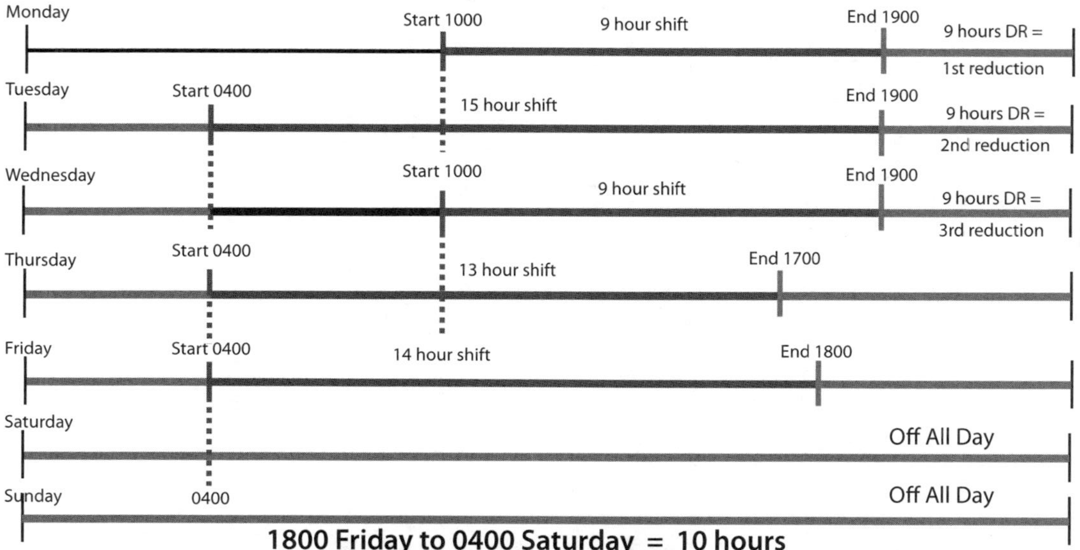

1800 Friday to 0400 Saturday = 10 hours

= 4th Reduction = GUILTY

Multi-manning daily rest periods
When multi-manning the drivers must take 9 consecutive hours rest in a maximum period of 30 hours.

When multi-manning, the first driver may now work the first hour on his or her own, thereby allowing the driver to collect the second driver, thereafter there must always be two drivers in the vehicle to permit the multi-manning regulation.

On the basis of this, if two drivers work together, the first driver can have a maximum 21-hour spreadover. However, the second driver in the scenario of meeting the second driver after one hour could only have a maximum 20-hour spreadover.

It is important to note that the latest tachographs automatically switch to PoA for the second driver when the vehicle is in motion. This prevents this time being recorded as a break. However, it is accepted by VOSA that where a vehicle is multi-manned then the first 45 minutes of PoA may be considered to be a driving break.

Ferry and Train Daily Rest Periods

When travelling by ferry or train, then the daily rest period may now be broken twice providing:

- the driver takes a regular daily rest period on these days (ie 11 hours or 3 + 9 hours)
- the two movements allow the driver to board and disembark the ferry
- no reductions are allowed when splitting the rest period with a ferry crossing or train
- the split in the daily rest is of no more than one hour in total and, therefore, includes boarding and disembarking; this one hour also includes all custom formalities — and does not count as part of the daily rest period
- during that regular daily rest period on a ferry or train, the driver has access to a bunk or couchette
- all the regular rest period is completed within 24 hours of work commencing.

This therefore means that for a driver to split the rest period by boarding and/or disembarking a ferry and allowing for no more than one hour of movement within the regular daily rest period, the driver should not have a spreadover in excess of 12 hours before beginning the first period of the daily rest in order then to complete the daily rest period of 11 hours in 24 hours when splitting the daily rest period with a ferry or train crossing.

Weekly Rest Periods

The law states that in any two consecutive weeks a driver shall either take at least:

- two regular weekly rest periods, or
- one regular weekly rest period and one reduced weekly rest period of at least 24 hours.

A *regular weekly rest period* is defined as 45 hours.
A *reduced weekly rest period* is defined as less than 45 but not less than 24 hours.

Where a reduced weekly rest period is taken, the reduction shall be compensated by an equivalent period of rest taken "en bloc" before the end of the third week following the week in question.

The law does allow compensation to be added to daily rest periods. Indeed, the law states that compensation must be made when adding to another rest period of at least 9 hours.

Therefore, if a driver was to take a weekly rest period of 24 hours at the end of, for example, calendar week 1, then there is a compensation of 21 hours (45 – 21 hours) to pay back and this must be paid back by the end of calendar week 4. When paying back the 21 hours, all 21 hours must be paid back at the same time in one block, and therefore, if adding to a regular 45 hour weekly rest period, the driver would have to take a weekly rest period of 66 hours.

Similarly, if the driver were to reduce the weekly rest period to 43 hours at the end of calendar week 5, they would have until the end of calendar week 8 to compensate.

Therefore the driver will have 2 hours (45 – 43 = 2 hours) to repay by the end of week 8. If during that week, calendar week 6, after the reduced weekly rest period, the driver was to take a 13-hour daily rest period, then this could be called 11 hours daily rest + 2 hours compensation and this would have paid back the reduction.

However, it is important to remember that even if the reduction is paid back, a driver cannot go two consecutive weeks without *at least* one regular and one reduced weekly rest period, and therefore, in calendar week 6, the driver is still required to have a regular weekly rest period of at least 45 hours.

When must a driver begin his or her next weekly rest period?

The law clearly states that a driver must begin his or her next weekly rest period no later than at the end of six 24-hour periods from the end of the previous weekly rest period.

This means when a driver resumes work at the end of a weekly rest period they can immediately calculate the latest time at which the next weekly rest must start.

This is simply done by adding six 24-hour periods on to the time work started after the end of the last weekly rest period as shown below.

If the driver starts work after a weekly rest period at 0600 hours on a Monday, then regardless of any shifts worked:
0600 Monday + 24 hours = 0600 Tuesday = end of 1st day
0600 Tuesday + 24 hours = 0600 Wednesday = end of 2nd day
0600 Wednesday + 24 hours = 0600 Thursday = end of 3rd day
0600 Thursday + 24 hours = 0600 Friday = end of 4th day
0600 Friday + 24 hours = 0600 Saturday = end of 5th day
0600 Saturday + 24 hours = 0600 Sunday = **end of 6th day**.

Therefore where a driver ends a weekly rest period at 0600 hours on a Monday the driver's next weekly rest must commence at or before 0600 hours on the following Sunday.

Emergency Exceptions

Provided that road safety is not thereby jeopardised and to enable the vehicle to reach a suitable stopping place, a driver may depart from the hours regulations to the extent necessary to ensure the safety of persons, of the vehicle or its load. A driver must indicate the reason for such departure manually on the record sheet of the recording equipment or on a printout from the recording equipment, at the latest on arrival at the suitable stopping place.

However, this does not allow a driver to derogate from the provisions of the regulations for reasons known before the journey commenced. In the matter of *R v Bird* [1996] R.T.R 49, ECJ, the court said this Article envisages only cases where it unexpectedly becomes impossible to comply with the regulation during the course of the journey.

INTERNATIONAL JOURNEYS

By way of EU Regulation 1073/2009, from 4 June 2010 where a driver is undertaking a single occasional service of international carriage of passengers, he or she may postpone the weekly rest period for up to 12 consecutive 24-hour periods following a previous regular weekly rest period (in other words at least 45 hours weekly rest period must have been taken before the international journey commenced and also, provided that:

(a) the international single occasional service lasts at least 24 consecutive hours in a Member State or a third country to which this regulation applies other than the one in which the service started

(b) the driver takes after the use of the derogation:

  (i) either two regular weekly rest periods (a total of 90 hours), or

  (ii) one regular weekly rest period and one reduced weekly rest period of at least 24 hours (a total of at least 69 hours plus the appropriate compensation at a later date before the end of the third week following the end of the derogation period).

Furthermore, under EU Regulation 1073/2009 two new regulations are introduced for international journeys from 1 January 2014.

After 1 January 2014, the vehicle must be equipped with recording equipment in accordance with the requirements of Annex IB to Regulation (EEC) No 3821/85. In other words these journeys must be undertaken using a vehicle fitted with a digital tachograph. Also after 1 January 2014, if driving during the period from 2200 and 0600 hours, unless the vehicle is multi-manned the 4½-hour driving period referred to in EU Regulation 561/2006 is reduced to three hours after which the appropriate breaks must be completed.

GB DOMESTIC DRIVERS' HOURS REGULATIONS

The GB Domestic Drivers' Hours Regulations apply to PCV vehicles used for the carriage of passengers on regular services where the route covered by the service in question does not exceed 50km.

A regular is one that carries passengers:

- at specific intervals
- along specified routes
- using pre-determined stopping places.

A 50km route length refers to a single journey length on service measuring the actual route taken.

Note: The GB Domestic Hours Regulations will apply to the majority of urban local services undertaken. Specific care needs to be taken with respect to the longer inter-urban journeys where the 50km route length may need consideration. In cases where a single journey route on a regular service exceeds 50km then this brings the service into EU rules.

Continuous Driving

When driving a vehicle under GB Domestic Drivers' Hours Regulations a driver can drive a maximum of 5 hours 30 minutes continuously.

However, this continuous driving period can be extended to a period of 8 hours 30 minutes providing the period includes total breaks of at least 45 minutes. Therefore, in a period of 8 hours 30 minutes there would be some 7 hours 45 minutes driving and 45 minutes of break. After this period of no longer than 8 hours 30 minutes the driver must either take a break of 30 minutes or begin a daily rest period.

Maximum Daily Driving

The maximum daily driving is 10 hours.

Working Day/Spreadover

The driver's maximum spreadover is 16 hours from when work begins to the time at which work ends.

Daily Rest Periods

The standard daily rest period is 10 consecutive hours rest, but this can be reduced to a minimum of 8 hours 30 minutes on up to three occasions in any one week, a week being defined as being from Monday to Sunday.

Fortnightly Rest

Under GB Domestic Drivers' Hours legislation a driver is not required to take a weekly rest, but must, in any two consecutive weeks take a rest of at least 24 consecutive hours; a week as stated above being from Monday to Sunday.

Therefore in a two-week period from Monday to the end of two Sundays later the driver must have taken at least one rest of 24 consecutive hours.

MIXED DRIVING

Some drivers may spend part of their driving time under EU rules and part under GB Domestic Regulations, possibly on the same day. The rules relevant to each portion of work should be obeyed, but EU rules apply to daily and weekly rest obligations.

Driving Limits

The domestic limits of not more than 5 hours and 30 minutes of continuous driving and 10 hours' daily driving must always be obeyed. But at any time when a driver works under EU Regulations the continuous/accumulated driving limit is 4 hours and 30 minutes.

Note: Driving under EU Regulations also counts as driving under GB Domestic Regulations, but driving under GB Domestic Regulations may be considered as "other work" under the EU Regulations.

Spreadover Times

Any driving under EU Regulations, even for only 1 minute, means that an EU daily rest should be taken both before and on that day and that an EU weekly rest is also required that week.

Recording Domestic Driving Under EU Rules?

If driving partly under EU rules and partly under domestic rules a driver should record all their periods of domestic driving as "out of scope driving".

This should be undertaken using the reverse of a tachograph chart when in an analogue tachograph vehicle or non-tachograph vehicle and should be recorded as "Other Work" with a comment explaining that this is "out of scope" driving.

When using a digital tachograph vehicle and undertaking "out of scope" work, use the facility provided. It is important that the driver takes the vehicle back in scope as the next journey may be under EU Regulations and each driver should select this option manually.

Alternatively, if the "out of scope" driving is undertaken in a non-tachograph vehicle and the driver's next vehicle is fitted with a digital tachograph, the driver can make a manual entry as Other Work on the driver card using the Vehicle Unit the next time the card is inserted.

ROAD TRANSPORT (WORKING TIME) DIRECTIVE — EC2002/15

Road Transport Working Time Directive (WTD) came into effect on 4 April 2005 and, in essence, all mobile workers who work under EU Drivers' Hours Regulation need to comply with WTD as well as EU Drivers' Hours and Tachograph Regulation as described earlier. This applies to all mobile workers who operate in vehicles which operate under EU Drivers' Hours and Tachograph Regulation, namely EC561/2006 and EC3821/85. For drivers operating under GB Domestic Regulations the Working Time Directive regulations differ.

As a brief overview the WTD introduces four limits.

1. Limit on the average weekly working time in a reference period (this excludes breaks and PoA).
2. Limit on the maximum working time in any one week.
3. Limit on the amount of work that can be done by night workers.
4. Limit on the amount of continuous work that can be done before taking a break.

The average working time for each week in a reference period shall not exceed 48 hours.

The reference period will generally be 17 weeks and this is covered later, but this can be increased to a maximum of 26 weeks if there is a collective or workforce agreement and the reference may also be changed to a rolling rather than fixed period.

In any one week the maximum working time can be increased, but it cannot exceed 60 hours' working time.

A night worker is anyone for who any part of their shift falls between 0100–0500 hours.

If any part of the shift does fall between these times then the working time (driving time plus Other Work) cannot exceed 10 hours in 24 hours from when work commences.

Furthermore, the operator will provide health checks for night workers.

For the purpose of the legislation a week is still 0000 hours on a Monday to 2400 hours the following Sunday, which is the same as that used for the EU Drivers' Hours and Tachograph legislation.

The legislation also states that all mobile workers shall have 28 days' annual leave entitlement.

This annual leave entitlement also, currently, includes the bank holiday periods. The annual leave entitlement and also time off sick cannot be used to reduce the average working time.

Therefore, where a driver is on holiday or sick then if the period of time off was one week holiday or sick the operator must add 48 hours to the working time for the reference period.

For each individual day off sick then eight hours should be added for each day.

The regulations will not apply to a driver who is considered an occasional mobile worker. It is possible that some of those who would consider themselves as non-mobile workers will actually fall within the confines of the Working Time Directive as they undertake in excess of the minimum amount of driving days permitted for occasional mobile workers.

Whether a driver is considered as an occasional mobile worker or not depends on how many days a driver undertakes work which would place him or her under compliance with the EU Drivers' Hours legislation. Therefore, it is possible that warehouse workers, fitters, mechanics and drivers who normally drive under GB Domestic Regulations may be mobile workers and therefore have a requirement to comply with the Working Time Directive, even when this driving under EU Drivers' Hours and Tachograph Regulation is on a non-regular basis.

Occasional mobile workers, ie those who fall outside the confines of the Working Time Directive for mobile workers, are those who:

- work less than 11 days under EU Drivers' Hours Regulation in a reference period of up to 26 weeks
- work less than 16 days under EU Drivers' Hours Regulation in a reference period of 26 weeks.

Therefore, if a driver operates in a vehicle which is under EU Drivers' Hours and Tachograph Regulation on more than the minimum number of days then he or she must comply with the Working Time Directive for mobile workers, there is no opt out from this.

In that case a system would need to be introduced to record, control and monitor their working time including non-driving days.

This information would also need to be stored for two years after the end of the reference period.

For those occasional mobile workers who are exempt from the Working Time Directive, ie they drive on less than 11 days in a reference period of up to 26 weeks, or drive less than 16 days in a reference period of 26 weeks under EU Drivers' Hours and Tachograph Regulation; they would still need to comply with the EU Regulation for Drivers' Hours and Tachograph legislation on those days they drive a tachograph vehicle.

More than One Employer?

If a mobile worker works for more than one employer, then he or she has a legal responsibility to inform all employers in writing of the other activity and the hours worked for the other employer — even where the second employment is outside the transport sector.

All of the work undertaken must be included when calculating the number of hours worked and therefore where two jobs are done both sets of work must be added together and, when combined, must still be within the permitted maximum average in order to comply with the Working Time Directive.

What Does Count as Working Time?

Refer to the *Work Modes* section on page 126, but for the purpose of the Working Time Regulations, the modes activities which come under driving and crossed hammers, count towards working time under the Working Time Directive legislation.

Maximum Weekly Working Time

This must be controlled to ensure that a driver does not exceed the 60 hours' working time (drive + crossed hammers) in a week. A week being between 0000 hours on a Monday to 2400 hours the following Sunday.

Continuous Duty

The Working Time Directive also brings in limits on the number of hours working time a driver can do without taking a break.

- At no time can a driver work more than six hours without taking a break.
- If in the course of the day the working time (drive + crossed hammers) totals between 6–9 hours, then a total of 30 minutes break is required.

- If during the course of the day the working time (drive + crossed hammers) exceeds 9, then a total of 45 minutes break is required.
- These breaks are regardless of whether a driver has accumulated 4½ hours driving.
- These breaks can be divided up into breaks of at least 15 minutes each.
- Therefore, after 6 hours a minimum break of 15 minutes is required.

Note: Also, breaks taken to comply with the Working Time Directive can be used to comply with the accumulated driving periods under the EU Drivers' Hours and Tachograph legislation and vice versa.

Working Time Directive for Occasional Mobile Workers or Driving under GB Domestic Regulations

These drivers are affected by four provisions under the 1998 Regulations.

1. Weekly Working Time: this must not exceed an average of 48 hours per week over the reference period (although individuals can opt out of this requirement if they want to).
2. An entitlement to 5.6 weeks annual leave from.
3. Health checks for night workers.
4. An entitlement to adequate rest.

Adequate rest is a very broad definition and VOSA guidelines, in PSV375, state that this:

> *"means that workers should have regular rest periods. These rest periods should be sufficiently long and continuous to ensure that workers do not harm themselves, fellow workers or others and that they do not damage their health in the short or long term".*

As with mobile workers operating under EU Regulation, this group of drivers can also amend their reference period for the calculation of the 48-hour average week. This is normally a rolling 17-week period, but can be extended up to 52 weeks, if this is permitted under a collective or workforce agreement.

TEST YOUR KNOWLEDGE

1. When driving on his or her own, under the EU Drivers' Hours Regulation what is the regular daily rest period required by a driver in 24 hours from when work begins, without taking a reduced rest period?
2. How many times, under EU Drivers' Hours Regulation, can a driver increase his or her maximum driving time to 10 hours in any one fixed week?
3. Under the Working Time Directive:
   (a) for how long can you work before you must take a break
   (b) what is the minimum that break must be?
4. If a driver takes a break of 30 minutes after 3 hours driving and then drives a further 1½ hours; what is the minimum break the driver must then take before commencing his or her next 4½-hour driving period?
5. For how many years is a driver's digital card valid?
6. What is the maximum number of days that a driver can go without downloading his or her digital card?

The answers can be found within Chapter 6 and can be checked on *page 223.*

7 RESPONSIBILITIES OF THE DRIVER

CUSTOMER CARE — UNDERSTANDING AND HELPING PASSENGERS

Disclosure and Barring Service (DBS) Checks

The respective roles of the Criminal Records Bureau (in checking individuals' criminal backgrounds), and the Independent Safeguarding Authority (in barring those with a criminal record from certain regulated activities) were merged, with effect from December 2012, into a single new non-departmental public body, the Disclosure and Barring Service. CRB checks are now known as DBS checks.

The **Protection of Freedoms Act 2012** revised the definitions of those regulated activities subject to enhanced checks and relevant to driving as follows.

- For children, those driving a vehicle transporting only children.
- For adults, those who transport adults because of their age, illness or disability either to or from their place of residence and a place where they have received, or will be receiving, healthcare, personal care, or social care; or between places where they have received or will be receiving healthcare, personal care, or social care.

Since 17 June 2013 the regulations have been further changed to remove the need for repeat checks. Once an individual has had a DBS check, and after paying a small annual update fee, the existing certificate can be reused and its validity checked online by the individual and by organisations.

Passenger Relations

Good driver/passenger relationships are an essential feature of a successful road passenger transport operation. A driver's relationship with the passengers will be good, and their custom will be retained, if he or she provides the service they want (and for which they are paying). Service and servility should not be confused — it is not necessary to be servile to deliver a professional service and keep the passengers happy.

The Driver's Image

Drivers should always be aware that they are generally the first point of contact between the passenger and the operator. Some passengers may have formed an initial impression of the service from the way they were dealt with when making a telephone enquiry or from speaking to an inspector, and certainly other employees have an important customer care role too, but the driver's role is paramount. Drivers can reinforce the first good impression or repair an initial poor impression and enjoy greater job satisfaction in the process.

Bus drivers are exposed to the public like actors on stage. Their behaviour reflects on the undertaking. Even when drivers are relaxing and talking amongst themselves, they must be careful not to be critical of their supervisors or colleagues within earshot of passengers.

Passengers observe the cleanliness of the vehicle, the way in which it is driven and the driver's timekeeping. A smooth and uneventful ride is not only the mark of a professional driver, it is also excellent for good customer relations as it confirms to passengers that they were wise to entrust their lives to you.

When passengers board a vehicle it is not usually with the express purpose of having a nice ride — it is because they want to arrive at a destination in safety and on time. But the quality of the ride can be either a bonus or a cause for complaint.

The price of arriving safely and on time is the fare which the passenger usually pays to the driver. Where the quality of service is perceived by the passenger to be poor he or she might be critical of the fares being charged.

Interestingly, passengers do not perceive off-the-bus sales of tickets in the same light, which is one good reason for operators promoting them — they can be good for passenger relations.

Not surprisingly, then, many driver/passenger confrontations arise at the time of payment (or when fare payment is being checked by an inspector).

Understanding passengers

To avoid confrontation as far as possible, drivers need to be able to understand their passengers. Many passengers feel insecure when boarding a bus or coach but try to hide their insecurity because no one likes to look foolish in public. This insecurity can arise in many ways. Passengers might:

- be afraid of boarding the wrong vehicle and need assurance that they are on the right one
- not know the fare to their destination and be afraid to ask the driver because he or she looks unfriendly
- be afraid of being late for an appointment or a connection
- have difficulty interpreting complex information on signs, bus stop display boards or timetables especially when services are changing
- have children or elderly persons "in tow"
- be young, elderly or disabled themselves
- become confused and be in need of your help — bus stations, airports and railway terminals can be confusing places and scenes of hectic activity.

Good passenger care simply involves recognising passenger anxiety, making allowances for irrational passenger behaviour and trying to be helpful and reassuring.

Product knowledge

Drivers must know their product, ie they must know the route, timetables and faretables, different types of tickets, passes and tokens and connecting services. They should be prepared to be asked questions and to answer them effectively.

Communication

It is the driver's job to communicate with passengers. Whether this is done on an individual basis or collectively (perhaps using a public address system), the rules are the same.

- Be prepared — drivers must know what they want to say. ("Engage mind before opening mouth" is excellent advice for all drivers.)
- Be calm — driving is a stressful job. Even if the passenger is ruffled, this must not affect the driver; it will do no good.
- Be assertive — drivers should not be bossy, just positive, so that there is no misunderstanding about what they are saying. If the fare is more than a passenger thinks it is, for example, the driver should show him or her the faretable; there is no need to apologise.
- Be concerned — most drivers show concern when a blind or disabled passenger boards their vehicle, yet many drivers fail to recognise the anxiety of travel.
- Be pleasant — a smile is free but can do more to win over passengers than all the advice given so far. Enquiry staff are often told by their employers to "smile on the phone". This is because, even though the people at the other end cannot see the smile, they can often pick up the warmth in the voice which accompanies a smile.

When things go wrong

There is little point pretending everything is fine when the passengers can see for themselves that it isn't. If drivers explain difficulties and delays passengers will usually accept the situation and may even be supportive. Drivers should keep passengers informed about what is being done to correct the problem. Passengers do not like being kept in the dark and can very quickly revert to a state of acute travel anxiety and begin to act irrationally.

Dealing with complaints

Because drivers are the initial, and sometimes only, point of contact between passengers and the operator, they must be prepared to receive their share of complaints. Some of these will be justified; others will be genuine but arise out of a misunderstanding or misinformation. A few will be unjustified.

Most, but not all, people find it difficult to complain. If passengers feel that they have a genuine complaint, they want to be reassured that it will be taken seriously. So drivers should always acknowledge complaints and report them using official report forms, when available. Obviously, if they can deal with the matter "on the spot" they should do so but if not, they should offer to pass it on to the person who can deal with it, or give the passenger details of how to make the complaint formally if he or she does not wish the driver to do so.

Most passengers will be happy for drivers to take up their complaints for them if they feel that the driver can be trusted to do so. It goes without saying that in order to deserve and maintain this trust the complaint must then be passed on. So it is a good idea to get a name and address or telephone number so that passengers can be contacted by the operator.

Summary

Drivers are the ambassadors of the company for which they drive. They are in full view of passengers whom they have to keep happy, secure and informed. To a large extent, drivers create their company's image.

RISK ASSESSMENT AND DRIVER HEALTH AND SAFETY

Risks

Driving buses, coaches and even minibuses or taxis requires the driver to be fit and healthy, alert and aware of the numerous risks that can affect him or herself, the passengers carried, other personnel in transport depots and bus stations, and the public at large.

There is always the risk of encountering angry, abusive and obstructive passengers as well as other road users afflicted with similar behavioural tendencies. Yobbishness can come in all ages — young school children, loutish teenagers, irate pensioners and frazzled shoppers — all of whom can cause headaches for the driver. Afternoon school runs, "going home time" and late evening services are particularly vulnerable to vandalism and unruly conduct and especially so with passengers who are under the influence of drink or drugs.

Throughout all of these occurrences, the driver needs to remain calm and composed and to assert him or herself only so far as is reasonable to retain control of the situation. Shouting at and verbal abuse of passengers, whatever their age or demeanour, is no solution. Invariably the employer has rules and workplace guidance on what to do in such circumstances and these should be followed rigorously if the driver wants to avoid being reported by passengers and penalised by his or her employer.

Misbehaviour on School Buses

Drivers may from time to time find that they experience disruptive behaviour when driving school buses. Many contracting authorities and operators issue specific guidelines to drivers, which should be followed in the instance of difficulty. General advice is to report instances of bad behaviour to the employer and the school at the earliest opportunity and, in instances of particularly disorderly behaviour, to stop the bus until order is restored, or to call the police in extreme cases. Drivers are best advised not to continue with a journey if they believe it is unsafe to do so.

Personal Injury

Where drivers suffer personal injury as a result of passenger abuse, through handling passenger luggage or other causes, they should report the details and circumstances to their employer as soon as possible so that an entry can be made in the official accident report book and appropriate management action can be taken.

Other Risks

Drivers face other risks besides those emanating from passenger behaviour. For instance, passengers falling or being injured when boarding or alighting from buses or when moving about when the bus is moving, when putting luggage on overhead racks or into the luggage storage area. In depots there are the risks from manoeuvring vehicles, vehicle exhaust fumes and from being in close proximity to other hazardous substances.

Driver health

Driving passenger vehicles is a tiring and stressful job. It needs the driver to keep him or herself fit and aware. Driving while under the influence of drink or drugs, besides being illegal, has an adverse effect on driver health, as can prescription medication which, among other things, can cause drowsiness especially on warm days. Missing meals and a poor diet also has a negative effect on driver fitness and keeping alert.

Driver stress

Whether through home or work situations, stress has an impact on the driver's ability to do his or her job properly, remain alert and aware of the potential risks of personal injury or road accidents. Stress can result in headaches, raised blood pressure and fatigue, which itself can lead to accidents and means that the driver is less likely to be tolerant of challenging passenger behaviour. Drivers who find that they are becoming stressed on a regular basis should seek medical advice.

CONDUCT OF DRIVERS, PASSENGERS AND OTHERS

Apart from the requirement by employers for their drivers to behave in a proper manner at all times when on duty, the **PSV (Conduct of Drivers, Inspectors, Conductors and Passengers) Regulations 1990** (SI 1990 No. 1020) as amended by SI 2002 No. 1724 (as amended) contain provisions which they are bound to observe.

Drivers must stop their bus as closely as is reasonably practicable to the left or nearside of the road when picking up or setting down passengers, and take reasonable precautions for the safety of boarding, travelling or alighting passengers (the latter provisions must also be observed by any conductor carried on the vehicle).

Conductors and passengers must not distract the driver's attention or obscure his or her vision while the vehicle is moving without having reasonable cause.

Drivers, inspectors or conductors must take all reasonable steps to ensure that passengers comply with the regulations. They must give particulars of their employer's name and address to any police constable or person having reasonable grounds for requiring it, and, in the case of the driver, details of his or her licence.

Smoking

Since 1 July 2007, smoking has been legally banned on buses and coaches used in the UK. "No Smoking" signs must be displayed in PSVs and drivers are responsible for enforcing the ban on passengers by acting responsibly and reasonably. Any deliberate infringement by passengers should be drawn to the attention of the operator or (if necessary) the police. (See *Removal of Passengers from the Bus or Coach*, p.162.) Failure to enforce the ban could result in a fine against the driver of up to £2500.

Microphones and Two-way Radio Communications

Drivers must not use a microphone or communicate with anyone directly while the vehicle is moving except:

- where it is essential to do so in an emergency or to deal with safety matters
- to communicate with a "relevant person" (the operator or an employee of the operator) on an operational matter so long as they can do so without being distracted from driving the vehicle (this provision permits the use of two-way bus radios)
- to indicate by means of occasional short statements the location of a vehicle when operating a service for hire or reward at separate fares (except an excursion and tour or sightseeing service) so long as they can do so without being distracted from driving the vehicle.

Passengers

In addition to the smoking ban (see above) passengers on PSVs must not:

- unless directed to do so by a driver, inspector or conductor, use any entrance or exit other than for the purpose which is indicated
- impede any boarding or alighting passengers
- endanger the safety of, or cause discomfort to, other passengers
- trail or throw anything from the vehicle
- distribute any printed matter which either seeks or gives information or seeks comment, or offer anything for sale, without the operator's permission
- give any signal which might be interpreted by the driver as a signal to start the bus or to stop the bus in an emergency

- travel in a part of the vehicle not available for carrying passengers
- use or play any noisy musical instrument (including a radio, iPod, etc) that may annoy other passengers
- refuse to leave the vehicle when instructed by the driver, conductor or inspector because:
  - the vehicle is full, or
  - the passenger has caused a nuisance, or
  - the passenger's condition is offensive to other passengers, or
  - the passenger's clothing is in such a condition that it might soil the clothing of others or the fittings of the vehicle
- deliberately interfere with the vehicle's fitted equipment.

Animals

Passengers with accompanying animals must comply with the instructions of the driver, conductor or inspector. If requested they must remove the animal from the vehicle.

Such a request must not be made of a disabled person in respect of his or her guide, assistance or hearing dog provided that sufficient suitable space is available for the dog(s) concerned.

Note: Assistance dogs will be identified by the jacket they must wear when they are providing "assistance".

Bulky, Dangerous or Cumbersome Articles

Passengers with such articles must comply with the instructions of the driver, conductor or inspector as regards where on the vehicle these are to be stowed. If requested they must remove the article from the vehicle.

Such articles will include those which:

- are bulky or cumbersome
- might be annoying to anyone on the vehicle
- might cause injury or danger to anyone on the vehicle
- might damage the vehicle or the property of a passenger.

Payment of Fares

A fare is defined in the regulations as an amount paid by a passenger that can be calculated by him or her from a faretable carried on the vehicle.

If requested, a passenger must state the journey he or she intends to take or is taking, and must pay the full fare for the journey.

Payment must be made either to the driver when boarding a one-person-operated bus, or on request to the conductor, or the passenger must use appropriate fare collection or ticket cancelling equipment.

The passenger must leave the vehicle when the journey for which the fare has been paid is completed, or pay the fare for any further journey. The regulations, in specifying the fare (not excess fare) for any further journey, effectively create the offence of overriding.

It should be noted that some operators have obtained statutory powers which enable them to charge a penalty fare in the event of a passenger failing to pay the correct, or any, fare.

Other operators attempt to achieve the same ends by including in all their faretables a hefty "standard fare" (in effect a penalty fare) payable in the event of the correct fare for the journey not being paid.

Tickets

As part of its plans to replace the existing Bus Service Operators Grant Scheme of subsidies based on fuel-duty rebate with a new scheme based on payments per passenger carried (ie an incentive per passenger (IPP) scheme) the Government is encouraging the replacement of paper tickets with a ticketing system using credit-card type smartcards with embedded microchips. The purpose of these systems is to provide audited data for the new IPP scheme. (See also *Smartcards* later in this chapter.)

In the meantime, passengers must not use tickets that are defaced, have been altered, issued to someone else and are not transferable, or that are expired. Any such ticket, or one issued in error, must be surrendered to the driver, conductor or inspector if so requested.

Any ticket issued for the journey (including pre-purchased tickets) must be retained by the passenger for the duration of the journey and be made available for inspection by the driver, inspector or conductor.

Removal of Passengers from the Bus or Coach

The driver, inspector or conductor may request the name and address of any passenger who they suspect of contravening the regulations and may remove from the vehicle any passenger who has contravened these regulations or may seek the assistance of a police constable who is then empowered to remove the passenger.

If the passenger refuses to give his or her name and address to the constable or fails to satisfactorily answer questions put to him or her for the purpose of checking his or her name and address, the constable may arrest the passenger without warrant (**Public Passenger Vehicles Act 1981**, s.25(2)).

Non-compliance with the regulations is an offence for which they may be liable to a fine at or below Level 3 on the standard scale of fines.

The Obligation to Carry Passengers

Operators have a legal obligation to carry all persons who present themselves for carriage in a fit condition at the proper place and time. A driver is not at liberty to refuse, without good reason, to carry any such person who is prepared to pay the fare and for whom there is room on the vehicle. A driver may, however, refuse a drunken, riotous or offensive person likely to cause annoyance or injury to other passengers and indeed would be in breach of his or her duty of care to the passengers were he or she not to do so.

The PSV conduct regulations, amended by virtue of the **Disability Discrimination Act 1995** and the **Disability Discrimination Act 2005**, place specific duties on the driver in respect of the carrying of disabled persons on local bus services (including school bus services when separate fares are charged to passengers by the service organiser) when operating "compliant" accessible vehicles. These obligations include:

- assisting wheelchair-bound passengers to board/alight and occupy a wheelchair space on the vehicle when available, and to operate any equipment provided on the vehicle for this purpose
- displaying and illuminating destination and route number indicators correctly
- allowing on board any "assistance dog" that is travelling with a disabled person — provided that space is available.

Note: Just because a person or passenger is disabled does not of itself constitute offence or annoyance to other passengers.

A "guide" to these extra specific duties and advice on complying with the Acts is available from the DfT.

The underlying principle of the two Acts is to allow people with disabilities to enjoy the facilities that are available without being disadvantaged, whether through cost, time or effort, as compared with a non-disabled person.

PSV operators normally apply standard terms and conditions of carriage but if these are so restrictive as to attempt to remove the operator's absolute liability for the safety of the passengers, the **Public Passenger Vehicles Act 1981** provides that they will be unenforceable.

Operators are liable, to those passengers with whom they make a contract of carriage, for their own negligence and for that of their servants. The contract is made by the passengers when boarding the vehicle, since this action is taken to signify their willingness to pay the fare.

In most cases the existence of a contract of carriage is obvious because the passenger buys a ticket and there is usually a statement such as "Carried subject to terms and conditions of XYZ Bus Co" printed on the ticket.

Of course, some passengers are carried "gratuitously", ie they pay no fare. However, the courts have held that such gratuitous passengers as pensioners or employees with free passes none the less have a "licence" to be on the vehicle and that the operator's liability under the laws of negligence cannot be any more restrictive than it can under a contract of carriage. (Drivers can be reassured that as employees they are further protected by their employers' compulsory employee liability insurance.)

An operator is liable for the safety of passengers' luggage carried on a PSV, unless the passenger takes charge of it. The driver's duty of care starts when the luggage is handed to him or her and continues until it is retrieved. He or she must allow sufficient time at stops for passengers to claim their luggage, especially where this is stowed in lockers only accessible from outside the vehicle.

Lost Property

Any person finding lost property on a PSV is required by law to hand it to the driver or conductor, or, if this is not practicable, to take it to the operator's lost property office (not to the police).

Drivers (or conductors) must where practicable search their vehicles for lost property at the end of each journey and be prepared to return any found article to anyone claiming it, provided they can be satisfied as to ownership. No fee (see below) is payable in this case. Otherwise they must hand it in to their employer for safe custody within 24 hours.

Operators have to keep a record of lost property. They can dispose of unclaimed lost property after a statutory period (usually one month but a shorter time for low value articles and perishable goods). A charge (not exceeding £2) can be made for the return of lost property. Official documents such as passports must be returned to their issuing authority.

Standing Passengers

The normal maximum number of standing passengers on a PSV is eight, or one-third of the seating capacity of the bus (or lower saloon in the case of a double-deck bus). However, smaller or larger numbers are frequently prescribed by certifying officers when a vehicle is given its COIF or Certificate of Conformity and these limits must be observed by drivers. In addition an operator may decide, or agree with staff, to carry a lesser number of standing passengers. The maximum number of seated and standing passengers or the number which the operator is willing to carry must be shown on the inside of the vehicle in letters at least 25mm high, which must also be visible from outside the vehicle.

Standing passengers are not permitted on:

- a half-deck vehicle
- the top deck or stairs of a double-deck bus
- any part of the gangway forward of the driver
- a PSV with 12 or fewer seats for passengers.

Seating Capacity

On PSVs with nine or more passenger seats the number of seated passengers must not exceed the seating capacity of the vehicle as marked (see *Standing Passengers* above).

However, in the case of children under 14 years of age, 3 seated children may count as 2 passengers. A child whose 14th birthday falls in a school term can be counted as a 14-year-old until the end of the school year in August.

The "3 on 2" rule cannot apply on any seats fitted with seat belts.

A child under five years of age not occupying a seat is not counted as a passenger.

Seat Belt Wearing on Buses and Coaches

The law requires that passengers be informed of the legal requirement to wear the seat belts (where available) whenever they are seated in any part of the vehicle and the vehicle is in motion. The methods of informing the passengers are through:

- the driver (where an operator chooses this method)
- the conductor, courier or designated tour leader
- audiovisual means (such as video)
- signs and/or a pictogram prominently displayed at each and every seating position where a seat belt is available.

Operators failing to provide the necessary notification face possible fines of up to £2500.

EU-wide rules effective since 18 September 2006 require passengers (except children under 14 years of age) and crew (eg courier) to wear the available seat belts when travelling on buses and coaches. Urban buses, ie those used in built-up areas entirely on 30mph roads or designed and certified to carry standing passengers, are exempt from this ruling.

ALCOHOL ON COACHES

Alcohol may be sold on buses and coaches provided that the vehicle concerned has been licensed for such purposes and that it is parked.

Alcohol may be consumed on buses and coaches by passengers subject to the operator's discretion and provided the passengers do not infringe the PSV conduct regulations (above). However, it is an offence for alcohol to be carried (even if not consumed) on a PSV travelling to or from a "designated sporting event" (see below). Operators, hirers and drivers are all liable if they knowingly cause or permit this to happen. Police have powers to stop and search a PSV if they think the law is being infringed. Heavy penalties with maximum fines of up to £1000 and possible jail sentences can be imposed.

Designated Sports Grounds and Sporting Events

The **Sporting Events (Control of Alcohol) Act 1985** and its associated regulations make it an offence for alcohol to be carried on PSVs used principally for carrying passengers for the whole or part of a journey to or from a designated sports ground or sporting event.

The following is a list of such grounds and events.

England and Wales

The designated sports grounds are:

- the home grounds of all football clubs that are members of either the English or Welsh Football Associations
- any other ground in England and Wales used by such clubs
- the new Wembley Stadium
- any ground not covered above used for any international association football match in England and Wales
- Shielfield Park, Berwick-upon-Tweed.

The designated sporting events concerned are:

- association football matches where at least one of the participating teams is either a full or associate member of the Football League or Premier League
- international association football matches
- association football matches in the UEFA Champions League (European Cup) or the UEFA Europa League
- association football matches that come within the jurisdiction of the Scottish Football Association
- association football matches that take place outside Great Britain where at least one of the participating teams either represents the English or Welsh Football Associations or is a full or associate member of the Football League or Premier League
- association football matches outside Great Britain where at least one of the participating teams is a member of the English or Welsh Football Associations competing in the UEFA Champions League (European Cup) or the UEFA Europa League.

Scotland

The sporting events concerned are:

- association football matches in the Scottish Premier League, Scottish Football League and Scottish Highland Football League
- association football matches in the competition for:
  - the Scottish Football Association Cup
  - the Scottish Communities League Cup
  - the Scottish Football League Challenge Cup
  - the Scottish Highland Football League Cup
  - the UEFA Champions League
  - the UEFA Europa League
- international association football matches in Scotland
- association football matches (not covered by the above) which come within the jurisdiction of the Scottish Football Association Ltd
- international Rugby Union football matches
- association football matches outside Great Britain where one of the teams represents:
  - the Scottish FA, or
  - a club which is a member of either the Scottish Premier League, the Scottish Football League or the Scottish Highland Football League.

FARES

On most local services and some longer distance services the drivers, unless they have conductors, are responsible for collecting fares and, usually, issuing tickets.

On some "flat fare" services passengers insert the correct fare into a glass-fronted fare box and the driver simply checks this and operates a lever to deposit the coins in a sealed vault. On other services with graduated fares there are "Exact Fares Please" and "No Change Given" notices, so that drivers do not handle cash.

On the majority of services, however, drivers issue tickets and give change.

Most operators now utilise electronic ticket machines (ETMs) that store fare values and details of tickets sold (which can then be downloaded to a computer at the depot).

Revenue Protection

The driver is responsible for protecting the operator's revenue. In some cases where a service subsidy has been won by tender the agreement may specify that the operator receives operating costs and the revenue goes to the tendering authority (Passenger Transport Executive or local transport authority). In this case the driver is responsible for a third party's revenue.

Inspections

For the reasons given above the bus may be boarded by an inspector appointed by either the operator or the tendering authority, who will wish to be satisfied not only that passengers are paying the correct fare but also that tickets have been issued properly and the revenue is being properly accounted for.

In other words inspectors are legitimately looking for both passenger and driver fraud and if a driver obstructs an inspector in the execution of that duty it could have the effect of jeopardising the service subsidy agreement on which the driver's job may depend. The operator might also view such obstruction as misconduct and take disciplinary action against the employee(s) concerned.

Waybills

The waybill is an essential accounting document which has to be reconciled with the cash taken by the driver. Depending on the ticketing system used, the driver may be asked to record the opening and closing serial numbers of pre-printed ticket stocks or the opening and closing cash register readings of the ticket machine.

ETMs record all or most details required on waybills and can automatically print relevant reports instead of waybills.

Data

Operators, and also tendering authorities who have to reimburse operators for concessionary fares taken and journeys made using off-bus purchased tickets, need to collect data relating to passenger journeys, mainly by ETM.

Some operators ask drivers to record intermediate figures on their waybills at each terminus for this purpose, others rely on data sampling by their inspectors or specially appointed data collectors. Drivers should co-operate with these staff when they board their buses.

Faretables

Faretables usually show the single adult fare between fare stages. Additionally, information on child fares, OAP concessionary fares (when charged), and fares for dogs and parcels will be shown. In some cases a fare code is shown so that when there is a fares revision new tables do not have to be created. Faretables can also be pre-loaded with most ETMs allowing drivers to reference these on the machine's display.

Typical Faretable (£s)

Service 427

Oldham Town Centre				
2.00	Clarksfield			
4.00	2.00	Lees High Street		
5.50	4.00	2.00	St John's Church	
6.50	5.50	4.00	2.00	Waterhead

Concession child (5–15 inclusive) £2.00

Parcels and dogs — half fare rounded up to nearest 50p

Typical Coded Faretable

Service 427

Oldham Town Centre				
A	Clarksfield			
B	A	Lees High Street		
C	B	A	St John's Church	
D	C	B	A	Waterhead

Concession Child (5–15 inclusive) = E

Parcels and dogs — half fare rounded up to nearest 50p

A = £2.00, B = £4.00, C = £5.50, D = £6.50, E = £2.00.

Tickets

Most "on-bus" fare collection systems involve the issuing of tickets and it is essential that drivers ensure that passengers receive a ticket whenever they pay a fare. This is a receipt for the passenger and proves entitlement to travel. The issue of a ticket also supplies data to the operator and enables cash takings to be reconciled.

Off-bus ticket sales

Some operators sell season tickets and multi-journey tickets through outlets such as railway stations, post offices and newsagents.

Multi-journey tickets are sometimes cancelled by validators on the vehicle or manually by the driver but electronic or Smartcard technology is increasingly prevalent in this area.

Most off-bus sales are designed to be attractive to passengers by offering a discount on bulk advance purchases of journeys, unlimited travel for a period (week, month or year) on season tickets, interavailability on other operators' services and special off-peak rates. They are also attractive to operators and drivers as cash is paid in advance and not on the bus and this speeds up boarding times.

Drivers should familiarise themselves with the availability by time and route of these various pre-purchased tickets.

Stage numbers

It is drivers' responsibility to change stage numbers on ticket issuing and cancelling machines as the vehicles pass the various stages. Unless they do so inspectors cannot check their vehicles for over-riders. On some electronically monitored bus service systems the stages are printed and charged automatically by the ticket machine.

Passes and permits

Many passengers, such as pensioners and scholars (children too old to qualify for child fares but still in full-time education) are issued with permits by operators and local authorities indicating their entitlement to concessionary or free fares either:

- in general, or
- at specified times, or
- on certain journeys.

Other passengers, such as some disabled persons, employees of the company and pensioners, are granted discount fares or free passes.

Drivers should be able to recognise the passes and permits that are valid on their buses.

Electronic ticket issuing machines

Most operators, including many minibus operators, use ETMs. These are speedy and simple to operate. They overcome many of the difficulties described above as follows.

- They contain a ROM (read-only memory) which is programmed to display the fare for any category of passenger between any two stages. The passenger states the destination and the driver enters the boarding/alighting points. The machine prints a correct value ticket.
- They also contain a module on which details of every transaction are captured. (It may be necessary for this purpose for drivers to issue "nil fare taken" tickets to holders of free passes or season tickets.) The module can be loaded by a driver and taken out when he or she leaves the vehicle. This not only obviates the need for completing a waybill, it also captures full passenger data for use by ticket inspectors and the operator. It can be read directly by a mini-computer which is then able to analyse the day's takings by driver, route and vehicle.

It is the driver's responsibility to collect this machine (or module if the machine is mounted permanently in the vehicle) and to return these at the end of the duty. This is especially important in view of the high capital cost of the equipment.

Smartcards

With this system of fare collection, passengers carry a credit card-sized personal plastic card containing either a magnetic stripe or an embedded microchip. This can act as either an "electronic purse" on which is stored a pre-paid value (like a telephone card) which is "decremented" when swiped through the driver's ETM, a travel entitlement or pass (eg for school children and some OAPs and disabled travellers with free passes), or a debit card on which information is exchanged between the microchip and ETM, sometimes with a contactless system (like the security gates in public libraries) capturing details of journeys taken and payments due. Drivers required to handle these systems will need to be trained to do so, although in most cases they work automatically with minimum driver involvement.

They are intended to speed boarding and improve travel data capture. The systems are in the main cashless, although some are designed to enable drivers to re-charge a smartcard to the value of cash offered.

Smart Ticketing

The Government has published its vision of a "smart ticketing" regime for public transport in England supported by integrated and innovative ticket products that can be purchased easily and quickly, leading to a significantly improved travelling experience for passengers. Eventually, it is envisaged, tickets will be loaded onto mobile phones instead of using smartcards, allowing people to buy their ticket, check timetables and real-time travel information, and view their stored tickets all on their phone. Low-value cash fares could be paid simply by tapping a bank card on a reader with no need to buy any ticket in advance.

More traditional smart ticketing products for things such as reservations and season tickets will be purchased online and downloaded before travel.

DRIVER'S DAILY WALK-ROUND CHECKLIST

Note: This walk-round check should be carried out by the driver on a daily basis. All items, where relevant, should be checked thoroughly and any defects noted must be recorded and reported.

Driving a vehicle on the road with defects is an offence which might result in prosecution and a fine and could lead to the loss of the driver's licence. The employer's "O" licence might also be jeopardised.

Check the following items daily:

- brakes (ie try before leaving the premises/depot)
- lights and indicators (ie all work correctly and lamp lenses are in good condition)
- tyres (ie no cuts or bulges are visible and there is adequate tread pattern)
- wheel-securing nuts/markers (ie no sign of loosening)
- windscreen wipers working and washer reservoir topped up
- horn working
- mirrors correctly adjusted and have no damage
- speedometer functioning correctly when moving
- analogue tachograph (ie time correctly set and chart inserted)
- digital tachograph (ie driver card inserted)
- number plates (ie undamaged and clean)
- rear and side reflectors (ie undamaged and clean)
- exhaust system in good condition
- speed limiter working effectively when the occasion arises
- current test certificate (if required)
- excise duty and "O" licence discs are valid and correctly displayed
- seat belts are in good condition (these must be worn if fitted).

CLEANLINESS AND FITNESS OF VEHICLES

Drivers should ensure that their vehicles are fit for use and clean when in use. In particular, vehicles should be washed whenever there is any danger of windows becoming too dirty for passengers to see out. It is especially important to ensure that the driver's windscreen is clean, the wipers and washers working and the screen wash bottle topped up. The vehicle should be swept out and seats dusted and vacuumed regularly. Any torn upholstery, worn floor treads or projecting fastenings or trim which could injure a passenger or damage clothing should be reported. PSV examiners are likely to prohibit the use of a PSV where the above points have been neglected.

Finally, the visual appearance of the vehicle, both inside and out is very important, as is the appearance and manner of the driver — this is especially so where competition allows passengers a choice of services. Even where a choice is not available a dirty vehicle or offhand driver and/or conductor can result in passengers seeking other forms of transport which could lead to the service being curtailed or eventually cancelled through lack of revenue.

8 ACCIDENTS AND INSURANCE

ACCIDENTS

One of the requirements outlined in the *Highway Code* (but never sufficiently appreciated by drivers) is the information that must be given in the event of being involved in a road accident. (The current 2007 edition of the *Highway Code* is online and available from most booksellers and newsagents, RRP £2.50.)

The following procedure should be adopted.

1. Stop at the scene of the accident.
2. If any persons are injured seek assistance and send for an ambulance and the police.
3. Try to obtain witnesses.
4. If you have been issued with a suitable mobile phone or camera, take photographs of the scene and the position of the vehicles concerned and of their occupants.
5. Exchange particulars with the driver of any other vehicle involved, ie:
   (a) the name and address of the driver
   (b) the owner's name and address if the driver is not the owner
   (c) the registration number of the vehicle, its type and colour
   (d) where there is personal injury the name and address of the relevant insurance company.
6. Record on paper (or the forms provided by your employer or insurance company):
   (a) the area and extent of any damage sustained
   (b) the time the accident occurred
   (c) where the accident occurred, ie:
      (i) the locality
      (ii) the names of streets and roads adjacent

(iii) the position of the vehicles at the time of the accident

(iv) the visibility and condition of the relevant road surface at the time of the accident.

(d) your assessment of the cause of the accident (include any information on whether signals were given).

7. Provide a rough sketch to emphasise the general situation.

All drivers obviously hope that they will not be involved in an accident and are therefore content to leave any consideration of this procedure until one occurs.

It is accepted that drivers, experienced or otherwise, may become nervous and excited when involved in an accident. It is essential, however, that the correct information is obtained at the time of the accident. (This is why the use of a camera can be extremely important.) Once the involved parties have dispersed the true facts can never be recalled. This is particularly stressed so that drivers appreciate the important role of factual information in negotiation between insurance companies.

When involved in an accident drivers must not admit responsibility for the accident to the other party or to witnesses; they should leave this for the appropriate authorities to decide.

It should be noted, however, that the law requires a driver to stop and report any damage caused to property on or adjacent to the road or injury to certain animals as a result of an accident, to any person having reasonable grounds for requiring such information including details of insurance. If this cannot be done immediately then the police must be informed as soon as possible and in any case within 24 hours of the occurrence.

In the context of the above, *property* means any other vehicle(s); street furniture, ie traffic signs, bollards, etc; garden walls; fences, etc. *Animal* means horses, asses, mules, cattle, sheep, pigs, goats or dogs.

Failure to stop or to report an accident is an offence and where reporting to the police is concerned this should be done as soon as possible; any delay (within the 24-hour period) may still bring prosecution if it is considered that the accident could have been reported earlier.

Accident Forms

It is customary for insurance companies to issue accident forms and drivers should see that they carry and understand one of these, as it will serve as a useful guide for obtaining the required information at the scene of an accident.

Company Procedures

In addition to the above legal requirements, many companies issue drivers with their own guidance on accident procedures.

The following is a summary of the more common procedures adopted.

The driver's first consideration should be for the safety and convenience of passengers. The driver is responsible for:

- ensuring that any injured passengers or other road users receive medical attention as soon as possible
- summoning the emergency services, if necessary, or making sure that this is being done
- trying to minimise the danger of any further accidents occurring as a result of the presence of his or her own and other vehicles involved on the road, by arranging for a competent person to direct other road traffic
- using a camera (where available) to record all relevant information regarding the scene of the accident and the position of vehicles and persons concerned at the time (whether injured or not)
- arranging for a "changeover vehicle" to be supplied so that uninjured passengers can continue their journey (this may also be done by arranging for transfer of passengers onto a following service vehicle if there is room)
- if possible, arranging for an inspector or supervisor to attend the scene of the accident to take statements from witnesses

- obtaining the names and addresses of any witnesses to the accident, whether bystanders or passengers.

Where the vehicle is in radio contact with the operator the above should not present any difficulty. In other cases the driver should use a mobile or try to find a telephone, reversing the charges if necessary.

INSURANCE

Compulsory Cover

It is legally necessary to have insurance cover in accordance with the Road Traffic Act "third party liability" for a PSV operator. The minimum insurance provides cover for personal injury and property damage sustained by third parties and "full" third party includes cover for loss to the operator through fire damage and theft. Upon the issue of a third party policy, a certificate of insurance is also issued, which confirms that the cover conforms to the Acts. This certificate must be produced (upon request) to a police officer, or, if this is not possible, within seven days at any police station.

The **Road Traffic Act 1988** requires that users of motor vehicles are covered against any liability which may occur in respect of death or personal injury to their passengers in the use of the vehicle on the road. All passengers must be covered and no "own risks" agreements are allowed.

Should insurance be required to cover accidental damage to the operator's own vehicle, it is necessary to take out a "comprehensive policy" which, apart from covering accidental damage, also embraces third party risks, together with cover for fire and theft of the insured vehicle.

The **Public Passenger Vehicles Act 1981** makes an operator absolutely liable for the safety of its passengers at all times while they are on the vehicle.

Production of insurance certificates

Where a driver is required to produce a vehicle insurance certificate at a police station, there is no obligation for the driver to produce it "in person"; the legal requirement is satisfied simply if the certificate is produced. The time limit for producing the document is "within seven days". However, if it cannot be produced within this period a defence is provided in the **Road Traffic Act 1988** (s.165) if it can be shown that it was produced at the police station as soon as possible, or, due to unforeseen circumstances, it was not reasonably practicable to produce the certificate before the day on which proceedings for non-production were started.

Note: New legislation introduced in 2011 under the new Continuous Insurance Enforcement (CIE) scheme requires that anyone who owns and keeps (not just who drives) a motor vehicle must ensure that either it is covered by current and valid insurance or is registered with the DVLA under the SORN scheme. Failure to do so is an offence and will incur a penalty. Uninsured vehicles will be clamped, seized and destroyed.

Road Safety Act 2006

This Act created, among many other new provisions, new offences of "causing death by driving whilst uninsured, unlicensed or disqualified" and "keeping vehicles that do not meet insurance requirements".

The Act also introduced new measures to deal with drink-driving, careless driving and inconsiderate driving. Many existing penalties are increased (ie to £5000 for careless driving and for failing to stop when required to do so by the police). Refusal to provide a specimen for laboratory testing, without reasonable excuse, means that the endorsement of the driving licence will remain effective for 11 years from the date of conviction.

9 DRIVING OFFENCES

DRINK AND DRIVING

Under the provision of the **Road Traffic Act 1988** (parts of which are amended by the **Road Traffic Act 1991** and further modified as regards drink-driving offences by s.14 of the **Road Safety Act 2006**) it is an offence to drive, attempt to drive or be in charge of a motor vehicle when having consumed alcohol in such quantity that the proportion of breath alcohol concentration exceeds the prescribed limit, ie 35 microgrammes of alcohol in 100 millilitres of breath (which is equivalent to 80 milligrammes of alcohol in 100 millilitres of blood or 107 milligrammes of alcohol in 100 millilitres of urine).

Penalties prescribed are, on summary conviction, a fine not exceeding £5000, or imprisonment for up to six months, or both.

On conviction on indictment, a fine or imprisonment of up to two years, or both, can be imposed (the maximum period of imprisonment on indictment for being "in charge" of a motor vehicle is one year). In addition, licence disqualification is usually imposed.

New breathalyser rules in France require all drivers to carry personal breathalyser kits. For France, the drink-drive limit is 0.02% breath alcohol content for PSV drivers and 0.05% for all other drivers (including freight), while new legislation in the Republic of Ireland (Eire) applies the 0.02% limit to all newly-qualified and professional drivers, including taxi drivers and goods vehicles, with a 0.05% limit for other drivers.

Breath Tests and Laboratory Tests

A police constable in uniform can require a driver to take a breath test at the roadside if:

- the officer has reasonable cause to suspect the driver of having alcohol in his or her body
- the officer has reasonable cause to suspect the driver of having committed a moving traffic offence
- the driver has been involved in an accident.

Failure to take the test, without reasonable cause, renders the driver liable to arrest and prosecution.

If a preliminary test indicates that the driver is over the limit, he or she will be required to go to the police station and unless he or she goes voluntarily the driver can be arrested without a warrant.

At the police station the driver may be required to provide two samples of breath for analysis by an electronic breath testing machine (which gives an instant print-out of breath alcohol concentrations) or a specimen of blood or urine for laboratory tests.

Failure, without reasonable cause, to provide a specimen of breath, blood or urine renders the driver liable to prosecution and the officer must warn of this prosecution when asking for a specimen. Under the **Road Safety Act 2006** (s.14), on conviction for this offence the offender's licence will be endorsed and this endorsement will remain on the licence for 11 years.

A statement automatically produced by the breath testing machine, a certificate signed by the police officer that the statement relates to the breath specimen supplied and blood and urine specimens, are admissible as evidence in a prosecution.

A blood specimen may only be taken by a medical practitioner and with the driver's consent.

Of any two breath specimens provided the lower must be used, except if the lower specimen shows no more than 50 microgrammes of alcohol in 100 milligrammes of breath, whereupon the driver has the right to replace the breath test with a blood or urine test.

The driver may be detained at the police station until the breath test indicates that the alcohol level is below the prescribed limit.

There is a statutory defence against being "in charge" of a motor vehicle if a driver can prove that, at the time, circumstances were such that there was no likelihood of him or her driving while over the prescribed limits or while unfit through drugs.

Where there has been an accident involving injury to a third party, the police have the power to enter any place where a drink-driving suspect may be, using force if necessary, both to breathalyse and to arrest that person.

DRUGS AND DRIVING

Driving while under the influence of drugs, whether prohibited drugs or prescription medicines, is also illegal and may lead the driver into a prosecution incurring a heavy penalty, including the potential loss of his or her driving licence.

At the present time, a conviction for driving while unfit through drugs requires evidence of impairment caused by the drugs concerned, but the Government is planning to further amend the 1988 Act in 2014 to the effect that, similar to alcohol, it will be an offence to drive or attempt to drive or be in charge of a motor vehicle with a specified controlled drug in the body, above the specified limit for that drug. The drugs concerned and their specified limits will be set out in the regulations.

It is proposed that penalties on conviction for the new offence will be similar to those attached to drink driving, involving imprisonment, fines and disqualification.

DISQUALIFICATION

These are offences for which:

- endorsement is compulsory unless there are special reasons
- courts have discretionary powers to disqualify

- if 12 penalty points are accumulated over three years, disqualification will result for at least six months. Once a period of disqualification has been imposed the existing points incurred under the totting-up procedure will be removed from the licence when re-issued to the driver concerned.

Where more than one offence is committed on the same occasion separate points may be incurred for separate offences.

The three-year period is a rolling term, ie it is measured on each occasion from the date the latest offence was committed.

When disqualification is imposed after the total number of points has been awarded, the period of disqualification will be:

- *six months*, if there has been no previous disqualification within the three years
- *one year*, if there has been one previous disqualification within the three years
- *two years*, if there has been more than one disqualification within the three years.

Disqualification can still be imposed for a single offence if it is considered to be serious enough and the liability to obligatory disqualification is retained for drinking and driving offences. (Drivers disqualified on conviction for drink-driving are subject to a minimum ban of one year for a first offence and three years for a second conviction for drink-driving within 10 years.)

OFFENCES FOR WHICH PENALTY POINTS ARE AWARDED

Courts may offer offenders the option to undergo training courses to reduce the number of penalty points awarded.

Courts disqualifying a driver for any of the specified offences below may order him or her to undergo another driving test before reissuing the licence.

Offence	No. of points
Contravention of temporary prohibition or restriction	3–6*
Use of special road contrary to scheme or regulations	3–6*
Contravention of pedestrian crossing regulations	3
Not stopping at school crossing	3
Contravention of order relating to street playground	2
Exceeding speed limit	3–6*
Causing death by dangerous driving	(a)
Dangerous driving	(a)
Careless and inconsiderate driving	3–9
Causing death by careless driving when under the influence of drink or drugs	(a)
Driving or attempting to drive when unfit to drive through drink or drugs	(a)
Being in charge of a vehicle when unfit to drive through drink or drugs	10
Being in charge of a mechanically propelled vehicle with excess alcohol in body	10
Failing to provide a specimen for breath test	4
Failing to provide specimen for analysis or laboratory test	(a)(b)
Motor racing and speed trials on public ways	(a)
Leaving vehicles in dangerous positions	3
Failing to comply with traffic directions	3
Failing to comply with traffic signs	3
Using vehicle in dangerous condition, etc	3
Breach of requirements as to brakes, steering gear or tyres	3
Driving otherwise than in accordance with a licence	3–6
Driving with defective eyesight, or refusing an eyesight test	3
Driving after making false declaration as to physical fitness	3–6
Failing to comply with conditions attached to a provisional or full licence	2

Driving following the failure to notify onset of, or deterioration in, relevant or prospective disability	3–6
Driving after refusal of licence or revocation	3–6
Driving while disqualified:	
– where offender was disqualified as underage	2
– where offender was disqualified by order of court	6
Using motor vehicle without insurance	6–8
Failing to stop after accident and give particulars or report accident	5–10
Failure of keeper of vehicle and others to give police information as to identity of driver, etc in the case of certain offences	6
Manslaughter or, in Scotland, culpable homicide	(a)

* 3 if fixed penalty
(a) 3–11 points if under exceptional circumstances disqualification is not imposed
(b) 10 points, depending on circumstances, if disqualification is not imposed.

OFFENCES FOR WHICH FINES ARE IMPOSED

Fines are imposed for:

- obstructing a certifying officer or vehicle examiner from inspecting a PSV, or from entering premises where such vehicles are kept, for the purpose of inspection
- driving a PSV or causing or permitting the vehicle to be driven, in contravention of a prohibition
- contravention of conditions attached to a PSV operator's licence
- failure to exhibit a PSV operator's disc on the vehicle
- failure to inform Traffic Commissioners of any relevant convictions when applying for, or while holding, an "O" licence or failure to inform Traffic Commissioners of material change in operating conditions of the holder of the "O" licence

- contravention of regulations providing for the control of number of passengers in PSVs
- failure to give notice to Traffic Commissioners relating to failure in, damage to or alteration of a PSV or other information relating to the vehicles in the operator's possession
- providing false information about PSVs in licence-holder's possession
- making false statements in order to obtain "O" licence, PCV driving entitlement or variations to such a licence or entitlement, COIF, type approval certificate, operator's disc or CPC
- contravention of regulations made under the **Public Passenger Vehicles Act 1981**
- failure to give the identity of the PSV driver in certain cases
- driving a PSV without a PCV entitlement or employing a driver without such entitlement to drive a PSV
- contravention of regulations as to conduct of drivers, conductors or inspectors of PSVs
- failing to produce driver's licence for endorsement
- contravention of regulations as to conduct of passengers in PSVs
- failure of persons carrying on the business of operating PSVs to keep accounts and records and to make financial and statistical returns
- forging and misusing documents appertaining to COIFs, "O" licences and discs, PCV entitlement, type approval certificates, CPC, a certifying officer or PSV examiner authorisation (fine and/or imprisonment)
- contravention of prohibition or restrictions of vehicles using roads of certain classes
- contravention of provisions as to use of special road
- contravention of weight limits on bridges
- contravention of pedestrian crossing regulations
- failing to stop at school crossings
- causing death by dangerous driving (imprisonment)
- dangerous driving (fine and/or imprisonment)

- careless and inconsiderate driving
- driving or attempting to drive when under the influence of drink or drugs (fine and/or imprisonment)
- driving or attempting to drive with excess alcohol in breath, blood or urine (fine and/or imprisonment)
- being in charge of a motor vehicle when unfit to drive through drink or drugs (fine and/or imprisonment)
- being in charge of a motor vehicle with excess alcohol in breath, blood or urine (fine and/or imprisonment)
- failing to provide a specimen for analysis or laboratory test:
  - where it was required for ascertaining ability to drive or proportion of alcohol at the time the person was driving or attempting to drive (fine and/or imprisonment)
  - in any other case (fine and/or imprisonment).
- failing to submit to a breath test
- speeding
- racing on the highway
- failing to heed traffic directions
- leaving vehicle in a dangerous position
- failing to stop after an accident or report the accident (fine and/or imprisonment)
- obstructing a vehicle from being inspected after an accident
- tampering with vehicles
- driving or riding in a motor vehicle and not wearing a seat belt
- driving a motor vehicle with a child in the front not wearing a seat belt
- driving a motor vehicle elsewhere than on roads
- prohibition of parking heavy commercial vehicles on verges and footways
- contravention of Construction and Use Regulations by using or causing or permitting the use of a vehicle adapted to carry more than eight passengers in that it is likely to cause danger:
  - by its general condition; the number of passengers being carried; the weight, distribution, packing or adjustment

of the load; the condition of the vehicle's brakes, steering-gear, tyres, or any description of weight; or its unsuitability
  - by the vehicle having an insecure load
  - in other cases
- using a vehicle without a test certificate:
  - when adapted to carry more than eight passengers
  - in any other cases
- using a vehicle that has been altered but not notified to the authorities
- using a vehicle without a certificate showing the type approval requirements applicable to it
- obstructing an examiner from testing a vehicle on the road
- failure of owner of defective vehicle to give certificate
- failure of driver of vehicle on roadside test to give particulars of the owner
- obstructing further testing of vehicle after a reasonable time following the issue of a defect certificate
- selling faulty vehicles or trailers or altering them to make them unroadworthy
- selling vehicle or vehicle part without required certificate showing type approval requirements applicable to it
- drawing more than permitted number of trailers
- allowing vehicle to be on the road without proper lighting
- driving without a licence or employing a person to drive without appropriate entitlement
- failure to comply with the conditions of a provisional licence or full licence treated as a provisional licence
- holding driving licence when particulars are incorrect
- driving with defective eyesight
- refusing to submit to eyesight test
- obtaining a driving licence when disqualified
- driving when disqualified (fine and/or imprisonment)
- failing to produce licence for endorsement and/or disqualification, etc
- applying for or obtaining a licence without disclosing current endorsements

- failing to produce licence to court making order for interim disqualification to committal for sentence, etc
- failing to produce to court Northern Ireland driving licence
- failing to give or provide evidence of date of birth or sex
- unregistered and unlicensed persons giving driving instructions for payment
- using motor vehicle without third party insurance
- failing to surrender insurance certificate to insurer on cancellation or to advise its loss or destruction
- failing to give information or making false statements on insurance claims
- failing to stop when required by a constable
- failing to produce driving licence to a police constable
- giving false particulars when stopped for careless or dangerous driving
- failure of driver involved in an accident, where injury to a person occurs, to produce evidence of insurance or report accident
- failure of vehicle owner to supply the police with information to verify the requirements of compulsory insurance
- forgery of licences, test certificates, insurance certificates, etc
- producing false evidence or making false declarations in order to obtain excise licence for vehicle requiring test certificate
- making false statements in connection with the remedying of vehicle defects found on roadside tests
- failure to notify the driving licence authorities of onset of, or deterioration in, relevant or prospective disability
- making false statements or withholding information to obtain insurance certificates, etc
- issuing false insurance certificates, test certificates, etc
- failure to attend public inquiry, give evidence or produce documents
- failing to attend inquiry when so ordered

- failing to attend or produce documents before a transport tribunal
- failing to comply with an "O" licence
- failing to keep records as to hours of work, etc
- failing to preserve records
- failing to produce records
- using a vehicle without an excise licence
- failure to exhibit an excise licence
- failure to observe the automatic half-barrier level crossing regulations
- making false entries on tachograph charts (fine and/or imprisonment)
- breaching the drivers' hours rules.

REMOVAL OF DISQUALIFICATION

A person who has been disqualified may apply to the clerk of the court that imposed the disqualification for the removal of the disqualification under the following conditions:

- if the disqualification is for less than four years, when two years from the date on which it was imposed have expired
- if the disqualification is for less than 10 years but not less than four years, when half the period of disqualification has expired
- in any other case, when five years have expired from the date of disqualification.

If the first removal application is refused, others can be made at three-monthly intervals.

If disqualification is for two years or less, application for the removal of the disqualification cannot be made. However, application to the quarter sessions for a reduction of the period can be made within 14 days of conviction and disqualification.

Courts disqualifying a driver from driving for any of the offences outlined in the above-mentioned schedules may order another driving test to be taken and passed prior to the reissue of the licence. A driving test cannot be ordered for any other road traffic offence.

If prosecuted for any of the offences listed, the driver must:

- submit his or her driving licence to the clerk of the court not later than the day before the hearing, or
- post the licence to the court to be received not later than the day of the hearing, or
- take the licence to the hearing.

REMOVAL OF ENDORSEMENTS

Endorsements are not removed from a driving licence until four years after conviction. For drinking and other driving offences the endorsements remain on the licence for 11 years.

DUAL LIABILITY

Both the driver or owner-driver and the employer are liable if any of the under-mentioned offences is committed:

- contravention of an order relating to street playgrounds
- contravention of Construction and Use Regulations:
  - in a manner likely to cause danger (vehicle overweight, insecure load, etc)
  - by breach of requirements as to brakes, steering gear, tyres
  - by driving while unqualified and employing and allowing a person who does not hold a licence to drive the type of motor vehicle in question
  - by the use of a motor vehicle uninsured or unsecured against third party risks.

An employer that permits or causes the vehicle to be used can also be prosecuted. Under the **Road Traffic Act 1988**, a defence can be made if the employer can prove that it did not know that the offence had been committed.

Corporate Manslaughter

Although not an offence that directly applies to coach and bus drivers, the offence of corporate manslaughter is one that involves the driver. This would occur where a driver's conduct on the road resulted in a death of a person as a result of negligent management or the failure on the part of the employer to exercise a duty of care in regard to the safety of persons (eg other employees, passengers, pedestrians and other road users).

10 USE OF VEHICLES ON THE ROAD

SPEED LIMITS

Speed limits in Britain are governed by the **Road Traffic Regulation Act 1984** and apply to roads and vehicles. Where these are different, the lower of the two applies.

General speed limits must be observed by all vehicles on the specific stretch of road to which the limit applies.

The maximum permitted speed on dual carriageways and motorways in Great Britain is 70mph and on single carriageway roads 60mph unless lower speed limits are in force for that road, or the vehicle is in a class which restricts it to a lower limit (see below).

Lower speed limits, usually 30mph, but lesser statutory limits can be imposed, applying to all vehicles on restricted roads that either have street lights at intervals of not more than 200 yards or are designated as restricted and have "repeater" speed limit signs erected. Where the 30mph limit has been increased or decreased on a specific restricted road this is indicated by appropriate traffic signs.

Mandatory speed limits (which must not be exceeded) at roadworks on motorways are shown as black figures on a white ground enclosed in a red circle, ie the same signs as used on restricted roads to denote speed limits.

Particular Speed Limits for Certain Classes of Vehicle

Class of vehicle		Motorways	Dual carriageways (other than motorways)	Other roads
1. A passenger vehicle with an unladen weight exceeding 3.05 tonnes or adapted to carry more than 8 passengers	Not exceeding 12m in overall length	70[1]	60*	50*
	Exceeding 12m in overall length or articulated vehicle	60	60*	50*
2. Dual-purpose vehicle if adapted to carry more than 8 passengers		70	60*	50*
3. A passenger vehicle, car-derived van or dual-purpose vehicle drawing one trailer		60	60*	50*

[1] Only older vehicles which pre-date the 100kmph speed limiter rules are able to achieve the 70mph motorway limit that is shown against class 1 (see *Speed Limiters*, p.64).

* Provided the dual carriageway or other road is not subject to a lower limit

Exemptions from Speed Limits

Vehicles being used for fire brigade, ambulance or police purposes are exempt from speed limits if such limits are likely to hinder the use of the vehicle for the purpose for which it is being used on that occasion.

LONGER VEHICLES

While this handbook assumes that all PSV drivers are appropriately qualified to drive their vehicles, many drivers may be faced with having to drive vehicles of lengths greater than those for vehicles previously driven. PSVs on rigid chassis can now be up to 15m in length (while so-called articulated "bendy buses" can be up to 18.75m long) and these require additional attention — especially to avoid collision by the rear overhang (out-swing) when manoeuvring from bus stops, parking places, etc and in confined spaces — particularly those not designed for vehicles longer than the previous maximum length of 12m.

Drivers of these longer vehicles should be on the look-out for signs restricting the operation of long vehicles, which may be erected by highway authorities where they consider that such vehicles present a risk to the safety of the public or other road users.

USE OF MOBILE PHONES AND/OR MICROPHONES

A mobile phone must not be held by a driver while the vehicle is in motion or even when the vehicle is stationary, if not parked with the engine switched off. Hands-on telephones may be used in an emergency.

"Hands-free" telephone systems may be used provided the attention of the driver is not likely to be distracted and the driver is in full control of the vehicle at all times.

Offences result in roadside fixed penalty fines of £60 and 3 penalty points endorsement on driving licences. If a case is taken to court, disqualification and a fine of up to £2500 could result if the defendant is found guilty (**Road Safety Act 2006**).

Note: The use of any type of microphone to provide commentaries while driving is forbidden under the PSV Conduct Regulations (see *Microphones*, p.159).

DRIVING ON MOTORWAYS

Motorways are designed for the purpose of permitting motor vehicles to travel at speed with safety, provided that the rules and regulations laid down are strictly obeyed.

Maximum safety will not be assured unless drivers using motorways are experienced in road procedure and lane drill.

Drivers must also be adept in handling vehicles at speed under prevailing conditions, which include "night driving".

Rules

A driver must not:

- drive anywhere but on the carriageway
- stop on the carriageway
- reverse on the carriageway
- stop on the central reservation
- stop on verges or hard shoulder, except in case of breakdown, accident or other emergency
- walk on the carriageway or central reservation, except in an emergency
- make a "U-turn"
- use the outer lane of a three (or more) lane motorway when driving a bus or coach of any weight that is constructed to carry nine or more passengers; this prohibition applies irrespective of whether the vehicle is fitted with a speed limiter or not
- disobey remote control signals, such as warning signals — Lane Closed, Maximum Advised Speed, and all other flashing amber light signals

- leave the motorway by an entry road.

Conduct on Motorways

- When joining a motorway (other than at its start) the approach will be from a road on the left (slip road). Give way to traffic already on the motorway, watch for a safe gap in the inside lane traffic, then accelerate so that the vehicle is travelling at roughly the same speed as the traffic on the motorway.
- Drive at a steady speed within the limits of the vehicle. On wet or icy roads, or in fog, keep the speed down.
- Driving for long distances can cause drowsiness. To help prevent this make sure there is a flow of fresh air in the driving compartment and suck sweets. When drowsiness occurs, turn off at the next exit or, if nearby, pull into a service area for a break.
- Exercise caution and drive well within the limits.
- Know the braking and stopping distances (see *Highway Code*).
- Extend courtesy to other road users.
- Do not "hog" the second lane.

HOV Lanes

High Occupancy Vehicle (HOV) lanes are to be found on some motorways. These lanes are reserved for the use of vehicles carrying two or more people — including buses and coaches.

Motorway Signals

Signals are used on many stretches of motorway and these are usually positioned at two-mile intervals on the central reservation and apply to all lanes. Variable message signs are now commonplace and warn of fog, ice, accidents and lane closures. On some very busy stretches overhead gantry signals are used for direction and lane separation information.

When the road ahead is clear the displays are blank, but in dangerous conditions amber lights flash and the central panel of the signal will indicate either in figures (which means a temporary speed limit) or symbols (arrows, etc) that a change of lane is necessary, or that the driver must leave the motorway at the next exit, due to an obstruction ahead.

The signals on overhead gantries, which are positioned over each lane, may also show a flashing red light which means that the vehicle must not continue beyond the signal in that lane. Similarly, if red lights flash on a slip road it must not be entered.

All signals should be obeyed since they are there to warn against danger ahead even though it may not be visible.

Driving in Fog on Motorways

- Before starting any journey in foggy conditions drivers should:
  - check that all lamps and reflectors are clean and that lights and indicators are working properly
  - clean the windscreen and windows and keep them clean by using wipers, windscreen washer and demister.
- It is essential to maintain a safe level of speed and a safe separation distance.
- There is an advisory speed of 30mph for driving in fog in the UK.
- Speed should be checked regularly as fog affects judgment of speed and drivers can easily find themselves speeding up without realising it.
- Fog makes tail-lights seem further away than they really are.
- Drivers should know the stopping distances of their vehicles and allow for these.
- Drivers should use headlamps or front fog lamps (if fitted) and rear fog lamps.

Prohibitions

Among the vehicles that may *not* use motorways are:

- cars driven by learner drivers
- pedestrian-controlled vehicles
- animal-drawn vehicles
- agricultural tractors, etc taxed at reduced rate
- engineering plant
- vehicles normally subject to a 20mph speed limit.

Breakdowns

1. If the vehicle breaks down get it on to the hard shoulder, if possible, and leave sufficient room for working on the offside. Use hazard warning lights.
2. If help is needed, use the motorway emergency telephone system to give an appropriate description of the vehicle and position. From the information in the documents carried give details of equipment, components or tyres, etc which may assist the police in correctly advising the breakdown services of the requirements. Before leaving the vehicle with passengers on board, give instructions to passengers not to leave the vehicle and, if possible, identify a suitable adult to take charge of the passengers until you return. For passenger protection purposes, passengers should, if possible, move towards the front of the passenger area of the vehicle until help arrives.
3. The driver should not wander away from the vehicle as the emergency control cannot call back, so if there is any undue delay a further call should be made to the emergency services.

Condition of Vehicles

Vehicle roadworthiness is essential at all times but before setting out on a motorway journey make sure that the following are checked and are in good order, as so many breakdowns and accidents are caused by the neglect of them:

- oil and water levels

- fuel
- fan belt (and spare)
- brakes
- tyres (condition and inflation pressures)
- driving mirrors, windscreen wipers and washers
- lights and reflectors
- steering.

PEDESTRIAN CROSSINGS AND BUS LANES

Zebra Crossings

Zebra crossings consist of rows of alternate black and white stripes between two rows of round or square-headed metal studs placed across the road and marked at each end by a yellow globe on a post containing a flashing light (Belisha beacon). In certain circumstances a constant light may be used.

On either the approach side or both sides of the zebra crossing (depending on local requirements), there is a "zebra controlled area" consisting of two or more white broken zig-zag lines, starting from short lines across the road and approaching the crossing, finishing at a dotted line (the give way line) 1m before reaching the row of metal studs edging the actual zebra crossing.

In the zebra controlled area overtaking is prohibited and vehicles must stop at the give way line.

Stopping in the controlled area or on the crossing is also prohibited except to allow pedestrians to cross, or in circumstances beyond the driver's control.

Pedestrians must be given the right of way if they are already on a crossing before a vehicle reaches it. On roads divided by a central reservation or a street refuge (island), each half of the road is treated as a separate crossing.

Pelican Crossings

Pelican crossings are controlled by lights and are operated by pedestrians. The difference between conventional three-light signals and the pelican signals is the flashing amber signal that appears immediately after the red as opposed to the red/amber signal. Pedestrians continue to have precedence on a crossing when the amber light is flashing but if no pedestrians are crossing vehicles may proceed.

Zebra crossing-style zig-zag markings also apply to pelican crossings and in the controlled area drivers are prohibited from overtaking a vehicle. Also they may not park or stop in the controlled area unless required to do so at the give way line.

Bus Lanes

Bus lanes on general purpose roads are provided for the improved reliability of bus and coach services and it may be an offence for other vehicles to enter these lanes when they are in operation (usually during peak hours). The lanes and permitted vehicles are clearly marked with special signs indicating times of operation.

A "bus" in the context of the regulations includes all passenger vehicles with more than eight passenger seats irrespective of their work and any other vehicles which are operating a registered local service.

Lanes marked by signs showing "Local buses" are for PSV use by only vehicles operating local bus services.

Red Routes

A scheme for priority route networks operates in London. Known as "Red Routes", double red lines marked on roads mean that vehicles are prohibited from stopping at any time, and on roads painted with single red lines stopping for loading and unloading is only permitted outside working hours. Buses may only stop at marked bus stops.

Fixed penalties for illegal parking on "Red Routes" are higher than for illegal parking on other roads.

PARKING RESTRICTIONS

- It is an offence to leave a vehicle unattended without stopping the engine and securely applying the handbrake.
- A vehicle and trailer must not be left on the road in such a position as to cause an obstruction.
- A trailer must not be left on a road detached from the towing vehicle unless the brake is set on at least one wheel or it is secured by a chain, chock or other efficient device to prevent the wheel from moving.
- Vehicles must not be parked opposite another vehicle or a traffic island.
- Vehicles must not be parked in a dangerous position, ie on a bridge, on a bend, within the studs of a pedestrian crossing, double white lines and clearways.

The following observations apply mainly to tour coaches and not to drivers of local services where stopping for passengers to alight or board is mainly at recognised bus stops.

Loading and Unloading Hours

Double yellow lines prohibit loading and unloading at all times. Single yellow lines restrict activity to the periods specified in the associated signs.

No Waiting and Parking

These restrictions are indicated by longitudinal yellow lines painted on the edge of the road. They do not prevent the picking up and setting down of passengers. Indeed, many local acts and orders permit vehicles to stand in "No Waiting" streets for this specific purpose and this is especially so in the case of the growing "hail and ride" urban minibus services.

There are two types of yellow lines:

- the solid single yellow line, which indicates "no waiting" during the times specified in the associated signs

- the solid double yellow line, which indicates "no waiting" at any time.

As with the kerb signs, the times of these bans will be shown on the lamp-post signs.

Note: In a "No Waiting" street drivers may only stop to pick up and set down. A police officer has the right to move drivers on.

Breakdown and Removal of Vehicles

If a vehicle breaks down in a prohibited street and must be left in order to obtain assistance, the police or traffic wardens should be notified.

The police are empowered to remove any vehicle that is causing an obstruction, contravening waiting restrictions or left in a dangerous position.

Parking Meters

Parking meters are included with the kerb marking signs that are displayed on discs to indicate the "controlled zone".

Double parking beside parking bays, etc which are already occupied is prohibited.

Civil Enforcement Officers (formerly Traffic Wardens)

Civil enforcement officers are empowered to enforce the following legal requirements:

- compulsory lights or reflectors
- waiting and parking restrictions by use of the fixed penalty system.

Fixed Penalty System

Fixed fines can be imposed without the case being heard in court. This system operates in towns and cities throughout the country.

Tickets (ie Fixed Penalty Notices) may be affixed to the vehicle or handed to the driver. In the case of endorsable offences the latter will apply as, provided the driver agrees to pay the fixed penalty, the driving licence will have to be surrendered for endorsement of the maximum number of penalty points. If the licence already shows an accumulation of penalty points that, with the latest offence, would bring the total to 12 or more, the fixed penalty would not be issued as the driver would be liable to disqualification. In these circumstances a prosecution would normally follow.

Where the driving licence is not immediately available the driver must produce the licence within seven days at a police station for the necessary endorsement to be recorded. A receipt will be issued, valid for two months, which will be acceptable in place of the licence if for any reason the licence is again required to be produced.

Fixed penalties are awarded for:

- using a vehicle without the required test certificate being in force — £200
- using a vehicle while uninsured or unsecured against third party risk — £120
- failure of vehicle keeper and others to give the police details of the driver, etc — £60
- non-endorsable offences — £30 (but see below)
- endorsable offences — £60
- parking on a "Red Route" in Greater London — £60 (or the sum specified)
- parking offences in Greater London other than on a "Red Route" — £40 (or the sum specified).

These are payable within 28 days or as specified in the notice. If payment is not received within the time limit the driver will be presumed guilty and the fixed penalty charge will be increased by 50% as a fine for non-payment.

A driver may either pay the fixed penalty or request a court hearing if he or she considers the circumstances to be wrong or unfair but in either case he or she must respond before the deadline, or otherwise be liable for the penalty and fine.

A new scheme of Graduated Fixed Penalties for UK drivers and foreign truck drivers was introduced from 1 April 2009. Under the scheme, police and VOSA enforcement officers can issue graduated fixed penalties to both foreign and domestic drivers for a variety of road traffic and vehicle offences including drivers' hours, overloading and the use of unroadworthy vehicles.

The fixed penalties range from £30 to £200 depending on the severity of the offence. In those cases where an offence requires court action and the driver cannot provide a satisfactory UK address, there will be a £300 deposit requirement per offence, up to a maximum of £900.

UK drivers who can show a satisfactory address have up to 28 days to either pay the penalty or choose to have the alleged offence heard in court. On-the-spot payments can be made in cash (ie GBP) or by credit/debit card.

Failure to provide a satisfactory UK address or non-payment of the penalty will be result in a prohibition being issued and the vehicle being immobilised until such time as the requisite penalty or deposit is paid.

Drivers are advised to always carry their driving licence with them to prove they have a satisfactory UK address. (They should also have their Driver Qualification Card (DQC) with them.)

Vehicle Emissions — Fixed Penalties

In addition to the fixed penalty system described above, the **Road Traffic (Vehicle Emissions) (Fixed Penalty) Regulations 1997** (SI 1997 No. 3058) and the **Road Traffic (Vehicle Emissions) (Fixed Penalty) (England) Regulations 2002** (SI 2002 No. 1808) allow specified local authorities, namely Birmingham, Bristol, Canterbury, Glasgow and Westminster City Councils, Middlesbrough Borough Council and the Council of the City of Swansea and County of Swansea, and any other local authority in England (covered by the latter regulations) designated as an air quality management area, to issue fixed penalties for vehicles exceeding emission limits. These councils may appoint officers, or any other persons who have successfully completed an approved training course, to test vehicle exhaust emissions and if the limits, as contained in Regulation 61 of the **Road Vehicles (Construction and Use) Regulations 1986** (SI 1986 No. 1078), are exceeded a fixed penalty notice for £60 may be issued.

The **Road Traffic Offenders Act 1988** provides for registered owners of motor vehicles to carry the ultimate responsibility for the payment of certain fixed penalty and excess parking charges when these have not been settled within the time allowed, ie 28 days. The liabilities relate to fixed penalties for:

- parking a vehicle on a road during the hours of darkness without lights or reflectors required by law
- contravention of waiting, parking, loading and unloading restrictions
- non-payment of a parking meter charge
- keeping a vehicle on a public road without a current excise licence.

Owner liability also extends to excess charges. Exceptions to these requirements are as follows.

- The registered vehicle owner shall not be deemed to be the driver if it is proved that at the relevant time the vehicle was in the possession of some other person without the owner's consent.
- In the case of hired vehicles (hired for less than six months) the payment of the relevant charges rests with the hirer and not the registered owner.

While the ultimate responsibility for the settlement of unpaid charges rests with the registered vehicle owner, this in no way absolves the actual driver.

The **Road Traffic Offenders Act 1988** extended the fixed penalty system to cover other traffic offences, including motorway regulations, speeding, failing to comply with traffic directions and various vehicle defect offences, etc and the complete list comprises:

- leaving a vehicle parked at night without lights or reflectors, as required
- waiting, parking, loading or unloading
- controlled parking zone regulations
- failure to display a current excise licence disc
- making "U-turns" in unauthorised places
- lighting offences by moving vehicles
- banned right turns and driving the wrong way in a one-way street
- contravening a traffic regulation order
- breach of experimental traffic order
- breach of experimental traffic scheme regulation in Greater London
- using a vehicle in contravention of a temporary prohibition or restriction of traffic on a road, ie where a road is being repaired, etc
- contravening motorway traffic regulations
- driving a vehicle in contravention of order prohibiting or restricting driving vehicles on certain classes of roads
- breach of pedestrian crossing regulations*
- contravention of a street playground order*
- breach of a parking place order on a road
- breach of a provision of a parking place designation order and other offences committed in relation to it, except failing to pay an excess charge
- contravening a parking place designation order
- breach of a provision of a parking place designation order
- contravention of minimum speed limits
- speeding†
- driving or keeping a vehicle without displaying registration mark or hackney carriage sign
- driving or keeping a vehicle with registration mark or hackney carriage sign obscured
- failure to comply with traffic directions or signs
- leaving vehicle in a dangerous position
- failing to wear a seat belt

- breach of restriction on carrying children in the front of vehicles
- driving a vehicle elsewhere than on the road
- parking a vehicle on the path or verge
- breach of Construction and Use Regulations*‡
- contravention of lighting restrictions on vehicles
- driving without a licence*
- breach of provisional licence conditions†
- failure to stop when required by constable in uniform
- obstruction of highway with vehicle
- using a vehicle without the required test certificate being in force
- using a vehicle while uninsured or unsecured against third party risks
- failure of vehicle-keeper and others to give the police details of the driver, etc
- using a mobile phone
- driving a vehicle without having a clear view of the road ahead.

Note: *Endorsement is obligatory in certain circumstances.
†Endorsement is obligatory.
*‡ This now includes the use of mobile phones while driving — see *Use of Mobile Phones*, p.199.

For most of these offences only police officers will issue fixed penalty tickets; civil enforcement officers will continue to deal mainly with parking offences.

Police officers are still able to warn drivers. In appropriate cases a police officer will issue a fixed penalty notice or, in more serious cases, prosecute in the normal way. Once a police officer has issued a fixed penalty notice the driver will have 28 days (or as specified in the notice) to pay. The driver still has the option to contest the offence in court and this is explained clearly on the fixed penalty notice. If the driver does not take either course within 28 days the penalty will be increased by 50% and enforced by the courts as an unpaid fine.

The fixed penalty tickets for the less serious non-endorsable offences are usually white.

The endorsable tickets are yellow and attract a higher penalty. Where a police officer has decided to issue a fixed penalty ticket for an endorsable offence the driver's licence with counterpart will be required so that the existing number of penalty points can be checked. A ticket will be issued and the driver asked to surrender the licence in return for a receipt, which will be valid for two months. If the penalty points for the present offence added to those which may already be on the licence total 12 or more — the level for disqualification — the driver will not be issued with a fixed penalty notice but will be reported for prosecution. A driver who is not carrying a licence will be required to take it to the police station of his or her choice within seven days. If a driver is stopped for an endorsable offence it will therefore be much more convenient if he or she is carrying his or her driving licence.

Penalty points for traffic offences are given under *Offences for Which Penalty Points are Awarded*, p.186.

Parking on the Road at Night without Lights

The **Road Vehicles Lighting Regulations 1989** allow vehicles to be parked on the road at night without lights in the following circumstances.

Motor cars, motorcycles and passenger vehicles adapted to carry not more than eight passengers may do so provided that:

- the road is subject to a 30mph speed limit, or less
- no part of the vehicle is within 10m of a road junction
- the vehicle is parked close to the kerb and parallel to it and, except in the case of one-way streets, has its nearside to the kerb.

On all other roads and in other circumstances the obligatory side and rear lamps must be switched on.

Passenger vehicles adapted to carry nine or more passengers excluding the driver, goods vehicles exceeding

1525kg unladen weight, and any vehicle to which a trailer is attached, must keep their lights (side lamps) on when parked on the road at night.

When lights are required on a parked vehicle two white lights must be shown at the front and two red lights to the rear.

It is illegal to use either a single parking light or a device that switches on only the offside front and rear lamps.

Parking in London

Part II of the **Road Traffic Act 1991** provides that contraventions of orders relating to designated parking places in London will no longer be a criminal offence and provision is made for authorities (Metropolitan Boroughs) to appoint their own parking attendants, "clamp" illegally parked vehicles and impose penalties (recoverable as civil debts). The Joint Committee of London Authorities appoints Parking Adjudicators to conduct a hearing in disputed cases.

With the increase in the numbers of coaches bringing commuters and tourists into the central area of London each day, congestion is inevitable especially when setting down or picking up passengers and when trying to park.

For the London Coach Parking Map go to the Transport for London website at *www.tfl.gov.uk/vcs/maps*. Further information is available from the Confederation of Passenger Transport (CPT) website at *www.cpt-uk.org*.

Congestion Charging

This type of "traffic management" was introduced in London in 2003. Buses and coaches are exempt from the charge under the London scheme.

Charging vehicles for access to parts of other cities is under consideration. A small-scale scheme was also introduced in Durham in 2003 under which only "local buses" fitted with a specific device are allowed access. Other buses and coaches are denied access and passengers wishing access can be set down at coach drop-off points or coach parks nearby.

ADVICE ON TAKING A PSV OUTSIDE THE UK

The key to trouble-free operation beyond the UK is to be thoroughly prepared and to ensure that the driver, vehicle and passengers all have the correct documentation required. (It is taken for granted that the driver will have maps and will have studied the route for the journey concerned, will understand the differing road signs and will drive safely in accordance with respective speed limits.)

The documentation and equipment which may be required for taking a PSV abroad are given below. The listing is not exhaustive and should be checked on each occasion to see whether a particular item is required for a particular country.

For the Vehicle

- Original registration document for the vehicle
- Copy of current annual test certificate for the vehicle
- GB plate mounted at the rear of the vehicle
- Waybill
- Service authorisation document (applicable for international regular services only)
- Insurance document and green card for certain countries
- Certified copy of Community Licence
- "Tempo 100" permit (for Germany) and vehicle rear "100 kph speed" marker (where applicable)
- "Vitesse 100" permit (for France) and vehicle rear "100 kph speed" marker (where applicable)
- Emergency warning triangles
- High visibility jacket for driver and other crew members
- "School Bus" signs (to be available if required)
- Snow chains (as required in the winter months).

For the Driver

- Passport (check for visa requirements for those with non-EU passport)

- National (EU) driving licence (for EU journeys) and International Driving Permit (for certain non-EU journeys — check beforehand)
- Letter from employer authorising driver to drive the vehicle on the journey concerned
- Tachograph charts for each day (sufficient for each driver and spares)
- Driver's card for digital tachograph (and spare print-out rolls)
- Letter of Attestation from employer (explaining any lack of continuity/gaps in the driver's tachograph records covering the working week(s) prior to the continental journey concerned)
- Fuel cards
- Two individual blood alcohol content breathalyser kits, Norme Française approved (French territorial requirement only — not needed if you access other continental countries via Netherlands, Belgium or Spain)
- Currency/credit cards.

For Passengers

- Passport (check for UK re-entry visa requirements for non-EU citizens)
- Ferry passenger list (must show name, sex and indication of age for each passenger intending to travel on a sea crossing).

Appendix

DEFINITIONS

AETR	European Agreement for Transport by Road Vehicles
ATF	Authorised Testing Facility
BSOG	Bus Service Operators Grant
CILT	Chartered Institute of Logistics and Transport
CRB	Criminal Records Bureau
COIF	Certificate of Initial Fitness
CPC	Certificate of Professional Competence
DBS	Disclosure and Barring Service
DfT	Department for Transport
DQC	driver qualification card
DSA	Driving Standards Agency
DVLA	Driver and Vehicle Licensing Agency
ETM	electronic ticket machine
gvw	gross vehicle weight
IPP	incentive per passenger (DfT's proposed new fare payment scheme)
ITA	Integrated Transport Authority
LEZ	low emission zone
LTA	Local Transport Authority
OCRS	Operator Compliance Risk Score
OFT	Office of Fair Trading
PCV	passenger-carrying vehicle (refers to the type of vehicle and defines a class of driving licence authorisation)
PSV	public service vehicle (refers to any passenger-carrying vehicle with more than eight passenger seats which is approved by the Department for Transport as fit for use in the carriage of passengers for hire or reward)
PTE	Passenger Transport Executive

RTSG	Regional Transport Services Grant (Wales)
TfL	Transport for London
TSO	The Stationery Office (source for copies of legislation, etc)
ULW	Unladen Weight
VOSA	Vehicle and Operator Services Agency

TERMS

Drop-back service	Practice of providing an additional vehicle into the normal vehicle requirements for a bus service, for a short period, in order to allow timetable recovery (departure time reliability) on services affected by traffic delays. This additional vehicle allows the other vehicles on the schedule to take increased layover time by "dropping back" to commence a later scheduled departure on time rather than continuing to operate late on the earlier scheduled journey
Interworking	Operation of vehicles or drivers which are scheduled on a regular basis to provide services by alternating between two or more bus services
Layover	Time within a bus schedule (running board) between the end of one journey and the commencement of the next
Roster (or rota)	List and pattern of duties (periods of work or "shifts") to be worked by a group of drivers. Drivers are allocated to a place on the roster (where the work is usually split into weeks) and then they rotate around the roster so that, over a period of time, each driver will work the shifts shown on each line (week) of the roster

Running boards	Driver instructions about the schedule for the vehicle on that particular working day
Spreadover	A type of duty or "shift" where the "on duty" time is spread in two or more short sections over the day — usually with lengthy breaks or rest periods in-between
Tidal flow operation	Practice of alternating the direction of priority for traffic according to traffic demand for road space

A note on speeds: the use of mph or kph in any regulation or control requirement on speed depends upon whether the "rule" emanates from UK regulations, in which speed is expressed in miles per hour (mph), or from EU regulations, in which speed is expressed in kilometres per hour (kph).

DRIVER CPC TRAINING REQUIREMENTS

The official EU Driver CPC qualification training requirements are presented in a combined syllabus covering both goods vehicle and PCV drivers, as defined by the categories of driving licence they hold or on which they are to be tested. The sections relevant to PCV drivers are extracted below.

This training syllabus, as set out in Directive 2003/59/EC (Annex I, Section 1, List of Subjects), indicates the knowledge to be taken into account when establishing the driver's initial qualification and periodic training regimes, which must include at least the subjects in this list. Trainee drivers are expected to reach the level of knowledge and practical competence necessary to drive all vehicles covered by their licence category both safely and with comfort for passengers.

The syllabus is structured under three key subject area headings, namely:

- advanced training in rational driving based on safety regulations

• application of regulations
• health, road and environmental safety, service, logistics.

The syllabus is printed below.

List of subjects

1. Advanced training in rational driving based on safety regulations

	Objective
1.1	To know the characteristics of the transmission system in order to make the best possible use of it: curves relating to torque, power, and specific consumption of an engine, area of optimum use of revolution counter, gearbox-ratio cover diagrams.
1.2	To know the technical characteristics and operation of the safety controls in order to control the vehicle, minimise wear and tear and prevent disfunctioning: specific features of hydraulic vacuum servo-brake circuit, limits to the use of brakes and retarder, combined use of brakes and retarder, making better use of speed and gear ratio, making use of vehicle inertia, using ways of slowing down and braking on downhill stretches, action in the event of failure.
1.3	Ability to optimise fuel consumption: optimisation of fuel consumption by applying know-how as regards points 1.1 and 1.2.
1.4	Ability to ensure passenger comfort and safety: adjusting longitudinal and sideways movements, road-sharing, position on the road, smooth braking, overhang operation, using specific infrastructures (public areas, dedicated lanes), managing conflicts between safe driving and other roles as a driver, interacting with passengers, peculiarities of certain groups of passengers (disabled persons, children).

1.5	Ability to load the vehicle with due regard for safety rules and proper vehicle use: forces affecting vehicles in motion, use of gearbox-ratios according to vehicle load and road profile, calculation of payload of vehicle or assembly, load distribution, consequences of overloading the axle, vehicle stability and centre of gravity.

2. Application of regulations

	Objective
2.1	To know the social environment of road transport and the rules governing it: maximum working periods specific to the transport industry, principles, application and consequences of Regulations 3820/85/EC and 3821/85/EC, penalties for failure to use, improper use of and tampering with the tachograph, knowledge of the social environment of road transport, rights and duties of drivers as regards initial qualification and periodic training.
2.2	To know the regulations governing the carriage of passengers: carriage of specific groups of passengers, safety equipment on board buses, safety belts, vehicle load.

3. Health, road and environmental safety, service, logistics

	Objective
3.1	To make drivers aware of the risks of the road and of accidents at work: types of accidents at work in the transport sector, road accident statistics, involvement of lorries/coaches, human, material and financial consequences.
3.2	Ability to prevent criminality and trafficking in illegal immigrants:

	general information, implications for drivers, preventive measures, check list, legislation on transport operator liability.
3.3	Ability to prevent physical risks: ergonomic principles, movements and postures which pose a risk, physical fitness, handling exercises, personal protection.
3.4	Awareness of the importance of physical and mental ability: principles of healthy, balanced eating, effects of alcohol, drugs or any other substance likely to affect behaviour, symptoms, causes, effects of fatigue and stress, fundamental role of the basic work/rest cycle.
3.5	Ability to assess emergency situations: behaviour in an emergency situation: assessment of the situation, avoiding complications of an accident, summoning assistance, assisting casualties and giving first aid, reaction in the event of fire, evacuation of occupants of a lorry/bus passengers, ensuring the safety of all passengers, reaction in the event of aggression, basic principles for the drafting of an accident report.
3.6	Ability to adopt behaviour to help enhance the image of the company: behaviour of the driver and company image, importance for the company of the standard of service provided by the driver, the roles of the driver, people with whom the driver will be dealing, vehicle maintenance, work organisation, commercial and financial effects of a dispute.
3.7	To know the economic environment of the carriage of passengers by road and the organisation of the market:

	carriage of passengers by road in relation to other modes of passenger transport (rail, private car), different activities involving the carriage of passengers by road, crossing borders (international transport), organisation of the main types of companies for the carriage of passengers by road.

This syllabus is reproduced here (with typesetting amendments for style purposes only) with acknowledgement to the European Parliament and Council in whose Directive 2003/59/EC it is published and under the terms of Crown Copyright Policy Guidance issued by HMSO.

Note for Readers

1. Certain legislative items have been updated since publication of this syllabus in 2003. In particular, under section 2.1 above, Regulation 3820/85/EC has now been superseded by Regulation 561/2006/EC of 15 March 2006, effective, in so far as the drivers' hours law is concerned, from 11 April 2007 while Regulation 3821/85/EC relating to tachograph use has been amended by this same Regulation, but effective in this case from the earlier date of 1 May 2006 when the fitment and use of digital tachographs first became mandatory in certain cases. Further information on these issues can be found in *Chapter 6* of this handbook.

TEST YOUR KNOWLEDGE — ANSWERS (FROM p.150)

1. 11 hours.
2. Twice.
3. (a) 6 hours; (b) 15 minutes.
4. 30 minutes.
5. 5 years.
6. 28 days.

INDEX

A

B

C

D

E

F

G

H

I

J

L

M

N

O

P

Q

R

T

U

V

W

Y

Z